Opening the American Black Box: How the U.S. Turned Its Monstrosity into Heroism
By Carmellini Duarte

Introduction Chapter: The American Dream and Its Shadow

The United States has always presented itself to the world as the "land of the free" and the home of limitless opportunities. A country where anyone, from anywhere, could transform their dreams into reality. This carefully crafted image is widely propagated through its pop culture, cinematic exports, and global political and economic influence. Nowhere else is the concept of "freedom" more embodied—or so it is claimed.

Yet behind this golden dream lies a shadow that cannot be ignored. A history of violence, oppression, inequality, and hypocrisy brutally contrasts with the idealized narrative of the "American Dream." From the extermination of Indigenous peoples and slavery to wars waged in the name of democracy but driven by economic and political interests, the United States reveals a dark side rarely displayed on the global stage.

The nation that proclaims itself as the bastion of freedom often curtails the rights of the most vulnerable. Beneath the sheen of advanced technology and promises of consumerism lies a system that perpetuates extreme inequalities, dismisses the poor, and exploits immigrants. At the same time, it promotes freedom of expression, often serving as a shield for hate speech and violence.

This book does not merely aim to expose the scandals and

monstrosities defining the darker side of American history. It seeks to dismantle the narrative that elevated the United States to the status of a global hero. By opening this "black box," we unveil how the country has turned its failures and dark deeds into heroism in the eyes of the world, masking its contradictions under the veil of exceptionalism.

The "American Dream" is, in many ways, a fable—but like every good story, it carries its share of nightmares. And it is these nightmares we must confront.

CHAPTER 1: THE 1929 CRISIS AND WORLD WAR II: THE TYRANNY OF PROFIT AND POWER CONSOLIDATION

Since its inception, the United States has built its narrative as the "land of the free" and the home of opportunity. However, behind this façade of prosperity and democratic values lies a history of unrestrained greed and geopolitical manipulation that negatively impacts the entire world. The 1929 Crisis and World War II are clear examples of how the U.S. used chaos and destruction as tools for its own profit and consolidation as a superpower.

The 1929 Crisis: Deliberate or the Result of Irresponsibility?

The Great Depression is often portrayed as an economic "accident," but many question whether it was an inevitable catastrophe or a manufactured crisis to serve the interests of powerful financial groups.

1. **Unbridled Greed:** In the 1920s, the U.S. experienced an era of extravagance, with rampant consumption and a stock market that seemed limitless. Industries overproduced while banks encouraged absurd levels of debt. This was not mere irresponsibility; it prioritized short-term profit over long-term stability.

2. **The Bubble That Had to Burst:** Some scholars suggest that the stock market was deliberately inflated by speculators who profited immensely before the collapse. When the crash occurred, the elite had already safeguarded their wealth, leaving the working class and foreign economies to bear the burden.

Even more alarming is the fact that, despite clear signs

of disaster, the U.S. continued printing money recklessly—an economic policy still reflected in its massive national debt, a burden ultimately passed on to the rest of the world.

Why Did Japan Attack Pearl Harbor?

World War II, initially centered in Europe, became a global conflict after Japan's attack on Pearl Harbor in 1941. But why would Japan, with no direct interest in the U.S., make such a bold move?

1. **Strategic Provocations:** Before the attack, the U.S. had imposed severe economic sanctions on Japan, cutting off access to vital resources like oil. This was not merely a diplomatic response; it was a calculated provocation to push Japan into war.

2. **A Perfect Pretext:** The attack on Pearl Harbor provided the U.S. with the excuse it needed to join the war and eventually position itself as the savior of the free world. Over the years, allegations have surfaced that the attack was deliberately allowed—or even encouraged—to justify American involvement in the conflict.

American "Aid" During the War: Profit Above All Else

When the U.S. finally entered the war, it was not just a combatant—it was a supplier. American industry flourished by producing weapons, vehicles, and supplies for the Allies. But this "aid" came at a cost. The Lend-Lease program was a profit-driven machine, charging already devastated Allies for support.

Hiroshima and Nagasaki: A War Crime Justified as Heroism

By 1945, the Allies were close to victory. Japan was already seeking to negotiate surrender, but the U.S. opted for a brutal display of power. The atomic bombings of Hiroshima and Nagasaki were not necessary to end the war—they were a warning to the world, especially to the Soviet Union, of American dominance.

1. **Cold-Blooded Targeting:** Hiroshima and Nagasaki were chosen not for their military significance

but because they were relatively untouched cities, ensuring the devastating effects of the bomb would be clearly demonstrated.

2. **An Unjustifiable Massacre:** Approximately 200,000 people died instantly or from radiation. Civilians became human test subjects for the most lethal weapon in history.

The Consolidation of American Tyranny

When the war ended, the U.S. emerged as the only intact superpower. The destruction of Europe and Japan became a springboard for American economic and political dominance. Under the guise of freedom's heroes, the U.S. exploited devastated nations, securing influence through loans and economic impositions.

Final Reflection: The American Dream or a Global Nightmare?

The 1929 Crisis and World War II reveal a troubling pattern in U.S. history: the ability to turn disasters—many of which it caused—into opportunities to consolidate power and wealth. Behind the veneer of heroism lies a story of manipulation, greed, and destruction that continues to shape the world today.

The U.S. may sell itself as the "land of the free," but the truth is that its rise to power was built on the ruins of nations it helped destroy.

CHAPTER 2: HIROSHIMA AND NAGASAKI – THE LEGACY OF DESTRUCTION AND THE NUCLEAR ARMS RACE

Details of the Attack: Destruction and Death

On August 6 and 9, 1945, the United States dropped atomic bombs on the Japanese cities of Hiroshima and Nagasaki. The explosions were devastating, transforming vibrant urban centers into apocalyptic landscapes within seconds.

- **Hiroshima:** At 8:15 a.m., the "Little Boy" bomb detonated 600 meters above the city, releasing energy equivalent to 15,000 tons of TNT. Approximately 80,000 people died instantly, with tens of thousands succumbing in the following months due to radiation exposure.

- **Nagasaki:** Three days later, the "Fat Man" bomb was dropped on Nagasaki. Despite the mountainous terrain limiting the blast's reach, the city was decimated. Over 70,000 people died by the end of 1945, with thousands more enduring radiation effects for years.

Beyond the immediate deaths, the attacks caused irreparable physical and psychological injuries. Severe burns, blindness, and radiation-induced diseases became a part of daily life for survivors, known as *hibakusha*.

LONG-TERM CONSEQUENCES

The destruction of Hiroshima and Nagasaki was not only a turning point in World War II but also a pivotal moment in human history:

- **Health Effects:** Subsequent generations faced alarming rates of cancer, heart disease, and genetic defects.

- **Psychological Impact:** Many survivors lived with profound trauma, enduring social stigma and the fear of passing radiation effects to their descendants.

- **Slow Reconstruction:** Both cities took decades to recover fully, becoming symbols of human resilience in the face of unimaginable tragedy.

THE ETHICAL QUESTION: WAS IT NECESSARY TO USE THE BOMB?

The United States justified using atomic bombs as a means to end the war quickly and avoid further loss of life. However, this narrative is frequently contested:

1. **Was Japan Already Defeated?**
   By the time of the attacks, Japan faced an unprecedented crisis. Its military was severely weakened, and there were clear signs the country sought to negotiate surrender, especially after the Soviet Union entered the war.

2. **A Show of Power?**
   Many historians argue that the bombs were not necessary to win the war but were used to showcase U.S. power, particularly to the Soviet Union, signaling the start of the Cold War.

3. **The Cost of Military Innovation:**
   The chosen targets—Hiroshima and Nagasaki—had limited military significance but were ideal for demonstrating the bomb's effects. Civilians became unwitting subjects in a grim experiment that redefined modern warfare.

SURVIVORS' TESTIMONIES

The accounts of *hibakusha* bear witness to the horrors of the attacks:

- **Setsuko Thurlow:** A Hiroshima survivor, Setsuko described seeing friends and family "reduced to shadows on the ground." She recalled the unbearable heat and the pervasive smell of burning flesh.
- **Keiji Nakazawa:** A boy at the time, Keiji lost his entire family and later recounted the psychological impact of witnessing charred and mutilated bodies while struggling to survive alone.

These testimonies remain powerful warnings for future generations about the horrors of nuclear warfare.

THE NUCLEAR ARMS RACE AND ITS LEGACY

The bombings of Hiroshima and Nagasaki not only ended World War II but also initiated the nuclear arms race.

1. **The Atomic Era:**
   The United States quickly came to see nuclear weapons as essential to its global dominance. In response, the Soviet Union launched its own nuclear program, culminating in its first atomic bomb test in 1949.

2. **Nuclear Proliferation:**
   In subsequent decades, other nations developed nuclear arsenals, increasing the risk of mass destruction. The "peace" achieved through nuclear deterrence has always been accompanied by the constant threat of global annihilation.

REFLECTIONS ON GLOBAL IMPACT

The attacks on Hiroshima and Nagasaki were not merely acts of war but statements of political and military dominance. They marked the beginning of an era where mass destruction became normalized as a geopolitical strategy.

The U.S.'s use of atomic bombs revealed a dark side of its power: the willingness to sacrifice innocent lives for political and scientific interests. Far from a heroic act, the bombings were a brutal demonstration of how the pursuit of supremacy can overshadow ethical and moral considerations.

CHAPTER 3: VIETNAM WAR – A BLOODY QUAGMIRE

Reasons for Entering the War and Fear of Communism

The Vietnam War, fought between 1955 and 1975, is one of the most controversial conflicts in modern U.S. history. Officially, the American goal was to contain the spread of communism in Asia, following the Truman Doctrine, which advocated supporting countries threatened by communist movements.

The U.S. viewed the war as part of the "Domino Effect," believing that if South Vietnam fell to the communists, other countries in the region, such as Laos, Cambodia, and Thailand, would also become communist. However, this widely publicized narrative masked deeper economic and strategic interests, such as controlling markets and strengthening U.S. influence in the Pacific region.

The U.S. supported the South Vietnamese government, which was unpopular, corrupt, and authoritarian, by providing arms, military training, and eventually sending hundreds of thousands of soldiers. America's entry into the conflict was marked by political manipulations, such as the infamous Gulf of Tonkin Incident in 1964, which was greatly exaggerated to justify military escalation.

Massacres and War Crimes: My Lai and Other Atrocities

The war was marked by brutality that shocked the world, and the My Lai Massacre, on March 16, 1968, became a symbol of the conflict's horrors. American soldiers massacred between 300 and 500 unarmed Vietnamese civilians, including women, children, and the elderly, in a defenseless village.

- **Summary Executions**: Civilians were gathered and shot, often after being brutally tortured.
- **Sexual Violence**: Women and girls were raped before

being killed in acts of extreme cruelty.

- **Complete Destruction**: Villages were burned and destroyed, leaving survivors traumatized and homeless.

The massacre only came to light years later when journalist Seymour Hersh exposed the crimes to the world. Even then, most of those responsible were never punished, highlighting the impunity that permeated the war.

My Lai was just one of many incidents. U.S. forces often treated the local population with suspicion and hostility, leading to similar actions in various other regions of Vietnam.

The Use of Chemical Weapons: Agent Orange and Other Atrocities

One of the darkest marks of the Vietnam War was the indiscriminate use of chemical weapons by the U.S., particularly Agent Orange, a highly toxic herbicide and defoliant.

- **Military Purpose**: Agent Orange was sprayed over large forested areas to destroy the vegetation cover used by North Vietnamese forces and the Viet Cong guerrillas. Over 20 million gallons of the substance were deployed during the war.

- **Health Impacts**: The substance contained dioxins, highly carcinogenic compounds. Millions of Vietnamese suffered poisoning, developing cancer, congenital malformations, and other chronic illnesses.

- **Impact on American Soldiers**: Many U.S. veterans were also affected, suffering severe health issues and passing congenital defects on to their children.

In addition to Agent Orange, the U.S. used napalm, an incendiary substance that stuck to the skin and caused horrific burns. Images of children running in panic, their skin burned, became global symbols of the war's cruelty.

The Quagmire and Humiliating Withdrawal

The Vietnam War was a disaster not only for Vietnam but also for the United States:

- **Human Cost**: Over 58,000 American soldiers died, and hundreds of thousands were physically or mentally traumatized. On the Vietnamese side, millions of civilians and combatants lost their lives.
- **Political Cost**: The war divided the U.S. like never before, fueling protest movements and public distrust in the government.
- **Economic Cost**: The conflict drained billions of dollars from U.S. coffers, worsening domestic economic problems.

The final withdrawal of U.S. forces in 1975, marked by the fall of Saigon, was an international humiliation. Images of helicopters rescuing Americans from the roof of the Saigon embassy symbolized the failure of one of the world's greatest powers against a small but determined country.

Reflections on the Villainy of the Conflict

The Vietnam War exposed the darkest side of American imperialism:

- A war justified by fear and paranoia but driven by geopolitical and economic interests.
- A war machine that did not hesitate to sacrifice innocent lives and destroy entire ecosystems.
- A nation that, instead of being a defender of freedom, revealed itself as an oppressor, imposing its will by force.

The scars left by the war remain visible, both in Vietnam and the United States. They serve as a reminder that, even under the banner of "freedom," the U.S. did not hesitate to plunge into the abyss of violence and destruction to preserve its interests.

Voices from the Quagmire – Accounts and Revelations of the Vietnam War

The My Lai Massacre Exposed by Seymour Hersh

Renowned investigative journalist Seymour Hersh played a key role in exposing the My Lai massacre, revealing the brutality of American forces and dismantling the U.S. government's official narrative about the war. His 1969 report detailed disturbing events that had been carefully suppressed.

Among the details exposed were the actions of Lieutenant William Calley, who ordered the massacre and participated directly in the executions. Hersh highlighted witness statements describing American soldiers shooting unarmed women and children, dumping bodies in mass graves, and burning entire villages.

Hersh wrote:

"My Lai was not an isolated incident. It was a symptom of a military culture that devalued Vietnamese lives, encouraged indiscriminate violence, and promoted a 'body count' policy where every death was seen as progress in the war."

The revelation was a shock to the American public, who had previously believed in the narrative that the U.S. was fighting for freedom and democracy in Vietnam. Hersh's report became a turning point in public support for the war.

American Soldiers' Accounts: Trauma and Reflections

Many American soldiers returned from the war deeply scarred by the horrors they witnessed and the actions they were compelled to commit. Veterans often faced post-traumatic stress disorder (PTSD), guilt, and social ostracism.

Paul Meadlo, one of the soldiers involved in the My Lai massacre, confessed:

"I killed women and children. I fired because I was ordered, but I will never forget. They were crying, screaming. I hear it in my dreams every night."

Another veteran, Ron Ridenhour, who helped expose My Lai, described the military mindset of the time:

"There was a culture of hate. We were taught to see the Vietnamese not as people but as 'gooks,' as if they were less than human. When you dehumanize the enemy, anything becomes possible."

The Suffering of the Vietnamese: Survivors' Testimonies

The Vietnamese people bore the brunt of the war, enduring relentless bombings, massacres, and the devastating effects of chemical weapons. Survivors' testimonies offer a harrowing perspective on the human impact of the conflict.

Pham Thi Phuong, a survivor of the My Lai massacre, recalls:

"I saw my mother and siblings killed in front of me. They had no weapons, posed no threat. I pretended to be dead, covered in their blood. I stayed that way for hours, not moving a muscle."

Another survivor, Tran Thi Hoa, who lived in an area contaminated by Agent Orange, shared:

"My son was born without arms. Many in my village have similar problems. This war continues to kill us, even decades after it ended."

The Brutal Logic of the "Body Count"

American military culture during the Vietnam War emphasized the "body count" as a measure of success. This approach, revealed in Hersh's investigations and soldiers' testimonies, encouraged indiscriminate violence. Many soldiers were pressured to inflate numbers, often killing civilians and presenting them as enemy combatants to appease superiors.

Hersh commented on this policy:

"It was a war where success was measured by the number of corpses. This created a system where humanity was lost, and Vietnamese civilians were the most harmed."

The Lasting Impact of Hersh's Exposure and War Accounts

The revelations of My Lai, survivors' testimonies, and veterans' accounts exposed the true face of the Vietnam War. The war not only destroyed lives but also eroded the moral credibility of the U.S., highlighting the hypocrisy of its rhetoric of freedom and democracy.

The legacy of the Vietnam War lives on, both in the physical and emotional scars of those who survived and in the lessons about the cost of war and the need for accountability. For many, My Lai and similar episodes serve as painful reminders that imperialism and war are inseparable from dehumanization and tragedy.

CHAPTER 4: WARS IN THE MIDDLE EAST – OIL AND POWER

The Fabricated Pretext: Weapons of Mass Destruction

The Iraq War, launched in 2003, was presented to the world as a mission of justice and global security. The U.S., under George W. Bush's administration, claimed that Saddam Hussein's regime possessed weapons of mass destruction (WMDs), posing an imminent threat. However, this justification soon unraveled as a sham. No WMDs were found, and subsequent investigations revealed that the decision to invade Iraq was based on manipulated reports and fabricated information.

Colin Powell, then Secretary of State, presented questionable evidence to the United Nations Security Council, including satellite images allegedly showing chemical weapons facilities. Powell later described his speech as a "blot" on his career, acknowledging the frailty of the evidence provided.

For many analysts, the true motive behind the invasion was control over Iraq's vast oil reserves and the consolidation of American influence in the Middle East. As former General Wesley Clark stated:

"Iraq was just the beginning. There was a plan to topple regimes in seven countries in five years. It wasn't about terrorism; it was about power and reorganizing the Middle East."

The Devastation of Iraq: Profit and Destruction

The invasion and occupation of Iraq plunged the country into chaos, resulting in hundreds of thousands of civilian deaths, the collapse of infrastructure, and a shattered society. While the Iraqi people suffered, American corporations profited from the war.

Defense contractors like Lockheed Martin, Raytheon, and Boeing secured billion-dollar contracts to supply weapons and military equipment. Simultaneously, companies like Halliburton, with direct ties to then Vice President Dick Cheney, profited from contracts for infrastructure reconstruction and oil exploitation.

A report by the Center for Public Integrity revealed that private companies earned over $138 billion during the Iraq War. Meanwhile, cities like Baghdad and Mosul faced blackouts, lack of potable water, and widespread violence.

Guantánamo: Tortures in the "War on Terror"

The invasion of Iraq was just one element of the "War on Terror," a global campaign launched after the September 11, 2001, attacks. Under this pretext, the U.S. adopted practices that violated basic human rights, with the Guantánamo Bay prison in Cuba standing out as one of the most notorious examples.

Prisoners accused of terrorism were held without trial and subjected to physical and psychological torture. Techniques such as waterboarding (simulated drowning), sleep deprivation, and prolonged isolation were routine. Leaked documents revealed that many detainees had no ties to terrorist groups but were captured based on inaccurate information or unfounded accusations.

Investigative journalist Jane Mayer, in her book *The Dark Side*, highlighted:

"Guantánamo wasn't about justice; it was about creating a narrative of strength and control. Torture didn't yield reliable information but perpetuated a cycle of hatred and dehumanization."

The Legacy of Wars in the Middle East

U.S.-led wars in the Middle East left behind a legacy of destruction, instability, and global distrust. Iraq, once a country with functional infrastructure, was reduced to ruins. Extremist groups like the Islamic State emerged in the power vacuum left by the American occupation.

Moreover, the fabricated justifications for war and the inhumane practices at places like Guantánamo exposed the hypocrisy of the U.S., which portrays itself as a defender of freedom and human rights. For many, these wars were less about global security and more about controlling strategic resources and projecting American power.

Conclusion

The Iraq War and the "War on Terror" are dark chapters in U.S. history. They not only caused immeasurable suffering but also revealed the country's willingness to manipulate narratives, exploit resources, and sacrifice lives for political and economic interests. The lingering question remains: who truly benefited from this devastation?

The U.S.'s True Interest in the Middle East

Fascination with the East: Oil and Geopolitical Control

Since the early 20th century, the Middle East has emerged as a key player on the global stage due to its vast oil reserves. For the U.S., ensuring access to this essential resource meant economic and military power. During and after World War II, strategic alliances with oil-producing countries like Saudi Arabia were established. Agreements such as the pact between Franklin D. Roosevelt and Saudi King Ibn Saud solidified American interest in the region: military protection in exchange for access to oil.

However, the quest for influence in the Middle East also involved interfering in local affairs, often disregarding the sovereignty of its people. Orchestrated coups, support for dictatorships, and military interventions shaped the negative perception of the U.S. among local populations.

Rising Hostility: Why Many in the Middle East Hate the U.S.

The resentment many Middle Eastern countries harbor toward the U.S. is not unfounded. It stems from decades of imperialist interventions and actions that destabilized the region while prioritizing American interests above all else.

1. **The 1953 Coup in Iran:**
   The CIA played a central role in overthrowing Iranian Prime Minister Mohammad Mossadegh, who had nationalized the country's oil industry. The coup installed the regime of Shah Mohammad Reza Pahlavi,

an authoritarian ruler who favored Western interests but brutally suppressed his people. For many Iranians, the U.S. was complicit in destroying their emerging democracy.

2. **Support for Israel**:
   The U.S.'s unconditional alignment with Israel has generated deep resentment in the Arab world, particularly regarding the Palestinian issue. Many countries and groups in the region view this support as a sign that the U.S. disregards the lives and rights of Arab peoples.

3. **Military Presence and Interventions**:
   From the Gulf War in 1991 to the occupations of Afghanistan and Iraq, the U.S. military presence in the Middle East is seen as a force of oppression, not liberation. Military bases, civilian bombings, and human rights violations have fueled visceral hatred.

September 11 and Its Roots

The September 11, 2001, attacks were one of the most tragic moments in American history. To understand their roots, one must examine U.S. actions in prior decades.

The group responsible for the attacks, Al-Qaeda, led by Osama bin Laden, originated from the Afghan resistance against the Soviet Union. During the 1980s, the U.S. funded and armed mujahideen groups, including Bin Laden, to fight the Soviets. This alliance, however, disintegrated when the U.S. established military bases in Saudi Arabia during the Gulf War—a move Bin Laden viewed as a desecration of sacred lands.

For the terrorists, the September 11 attacks were a direct retaliation against American foreign policy. Military presence, support for Israel, and imperialist interventions were cited as reasons for the attack.

Conclusion: Oil, Power, and Blood

The Middle East stands as a testament to the devastating impact of American interventionism. By prioritizing oil and geopolitical power, the U.S. has undermined governments, divided societies, and fostered hatred that endures to this day. The echoing question is: how much longer will the region pay the price for America's imperialist ambitions?

CHAPTER 5: KOREAN WAR – THE CONFLICT WITHOUT VICTORY

1. Historical Context and the Division of the Peninsula

The Korean War, which began in 1950, serves as a stark example of the United States' aggressive and ambiguous global policies. The Korean Peninsula was divided after World War II in 1945 between Soviet and American forces, leading to the emergence of two distinct states:

- **North Korea:** Under a communist regime supported by the Soviet Union.
- **South Korea:** Under a capitalist government allied with the U.S., aimed at containing the spread of communism in Asia.

The United States entered the Korean War under the pretext of defending South Korea from communist expansion. However, the war revealed how the U.S. was willing to sacrifice lives and resources, often driven by political and ideological strategies, without achieving a decisive or lasting victory.

2. U.S. INVOLVEMENT AND THE DYNAMICS OF THE CONFLICT

The early years of the conflict showcased U.S. military strength but also its inability to secure a decisive outcome.

- **Mass Mobilization:** The U.S. support for South Korea involved deploying over 500,000 American troops, alongside substantial material and financial resources, including aircraft, tanks, and heavy equipment.
- **Unstable Frontlines:** Despite its military power, the U.S. faced fierce resistance from North Korean forces, backed by China, making any decisive victory nearly impossible.
- **Americanized Strategy:** The conflict highlighted the U.S. approach of relying on brute force and technical power without considering the social and political impacts on the ground. The objective was not only to win but to curb communism—a strategy with complex economic and political implications.

3. THE HUMAN AND SOCIAL COST OF WAR

The Korean War resulted in significant casualties and widespread suffering, impacting both American soldiers and Korean civilians.

- **Casualties and Missing Persons:** Approximately 36,000 American soldiers lost their lives, while Korean deaths—on both sides—were even more alarming, with an estimated 2 million fatalities.

- **Widespread Destruction:** Entire cities were devastated, and infrastructure in both North and South Korea suffered severe damage. Post-war reconstruction was hindered by extreme poverty and ruins.

- **Psychological Trauma:** Many American and Korean soldiers endured physical and emotional scars. The indiscriminate use of force and intense battles left profound mental health and societal challenges that persist today.

4. GEOPOLITICAL RIVALRIES AND THE INFLUENCE OF FOREIGN POWERS

The Korean War not only shaped the peninsula but also redefined the global balance of power between Western and communist blocs.

- **U.S. Interventionism:** The U.S. involvement aimed to contain communism while solidifying its military presence in East Asia. American bases in Seoul and the strategic positioning of troops remain symbolic of this influence.

- **China's Role:** China's intervention to support North Korea was pivotal. It demonstrated the communist government's commitment to global communism and its growing influence in Asia, fueling ongoing tensions with the U.S.

- **Soviet Union's Support:** The Soviet Union played a key role by providing resources and support to North Korea, making the Korean War a proxy battle of the Cold War ideological clash between capitalism and communism.

5. LASTING CONSEQUENCES AND THE ARMISTICE

The war ended in 1953 with an armistice, but no formal peace treaty was signed, leaving North and South Korea technically at war.

- **Demilitarized Zone (DMZ):** One significant outcome was the creation of the heavily guarded and monitored DMZ, symbolizing the physical and ideological separation of the two nations and their state of constant tension.
- **Tense Bilateral Relations:** Despite promises of agreements and diplomatic discussions, relations between North and South Korea, as well as between the U.S. and North Korea, remain unstable.
- **American Influence:** The U.S. presence in Korea remains a cornerstone of South Korea's defense strategy but also a source of international tension and political pressure in Asia and at home.

6. THE HYPOCRISY OF U.S. POLITICAL DECISIONS

The U.S., which often claims to fight wars in the name of human rights, faced criticism during the Korean War for the disparity between rhetoric and practice.

- **Protection from Communism:** While the stated goal was to protect South Koreans from communism, the U.S. methods caused immense destruction and suffering, raising questions about the efficacy of their intervention.
- **Arms Industry Profits:** The war bolstered the U.S. arms industry, demonstrating how conflicts are often driven by economic interests rather than solely political or social ideals.

CONCLUSION

The Korean War is a brutal example of American policies driven by ideological interests. While the U.S. aimed to contain communism and support South Korea, the conflict underscored the cost of military interventionism, strategic decisions motivated by economic and ideological power, and disregard for the social and economic impacts on the war-torn countries.

To this day, the remnants of the war linger in the Korean DMZ, regional instability, and complex relations between Asian and Western powers. The United States' commitment to ideological and economic interests often outweighs its commitment to the people, making the Korean War a landmark of decisions revealing its pursuit of global influence and control—no matter the cost.

SOUTH KOREA: A DISGUISED U.S. COLONY?

The notion that South Korea is, in some ways, a "colony" of the United States is not merely theoretical. Despite its formal sovereignty, the deep and complex relationship between the two nations reveals aspects that draw this critical comparison.

1. Historical and U.S. Influence

- **Permanent Military Presence:** Since the Korean War ended in 1953, the U.S. has maintained a significant military presence in South Korea.

    - **American Troops Base:** Approximately 28,500 American soldiers are currently stationed in South Korea, in strategic locations such as near Seoul and bases south of the DMZ.

    - **Joint Command:** U.S. forces operate under the Combined Forces Command, highlighting American control over military operations and defense strategies in the region.

    - **Security Agreement:** The U.S.-South Korea security pact obliges American military support, including advanced equipment and troop deployment.

2. Economic and Political Dependence

- **Economic Partnerships:** The U.S. is a major trade partner for South Korea, exporting electronics, automobiles, and other goods while hosting significant American corporate investments.

- **Foreign Investments:** South Korean companies rely on U.S. markets and capital investments, creating an intertwined economic dependency.

- **Bilateral Agreements:** The U.S.-Korea Free Trade Agreement (KORUS FTA) solidifies these economic ties, further deepening the reliance.

3. Cultural and Social Aspects

- **Americanization:** Since the 1950s, U.S. military and economic presence has significantly influenced South Korean culture. American pop music, movies, fashion, and food are prevalent, especially among younger generations.
- **Media Influence:** American films, TV shows, and music play a major role in shaping societal norms and aspirations.

4. Strategic Challenges

Despite its formal independence, South Korea's reliance on the U.S. raises critical questions about its sovereignty. Voices within South Korea advocate for greater autonomy, diversifying alliances, and lessening dependence on American influence to foster a truly independent path.

CHAPTER 6: MILITARY INTERVENTIONS AND SUPPORT FOR DICTATORSHIPS IN LATIN AMERICA

1. The Context of U.S. Interventions in Latin America

Since the early 20th century, the United States has played a central role in the politics and internal conflicts of Latin America through both direct military interventions and support for dictatorial regimes. U.S. interest in the region arose not only from economic and strategic motives but also from its vision of political control and regional influence, aiming to counter communism and protect American investments in companies and natural resources.

2. The Monroe Doctrine and American Influence

Historical Origins

The foundation of U.S. interventions in Latin America lies in the Monroe Doctrine, proclaimed in 1823, which stated that the U.S. would not tolerate European interference in the Western Hemisphere.

- **Strategic Objective:** The Monroe Doctrine became a justification for military interventions and support for governments that secured American interests in the continent.

- **Economic and Geopolitical Interest:** It ensured access to natural resources, markets, and military power, establishing the U.S. as the dominant figure in Latin American geopolitics.

3. The Role of Direct Military Interventions

Panama and the Separation

- **Objective:** In 1903, the U.S. supported Panama's independence from Colombia to gain control over the

Panama Canal, a crucial strategic route for trade and defense of American interests.

- **Consequences:** U.S. military and political support ensured decades-long control over the canal, despite international criticism and tensions.

Interventions in Haiti and the Dominican Republic

Between 1915 and 1934, the U.S. occupied Haiti and the Dominican Republic to protect American investments and install governments favorable to trade and economic interests.

- **Outcomes:** These governments led to resource exploitation and economic subjugation but also political and social repression, with many citizens suffering violence and poverty.

4. Support for Dictatorships During the Cold War

During the Cold War, U.S. policy in Latin America focused on combating communism and Soviet influence in the region. This often meant supporting military dictatorships, even when those regimes committed repression and human rights violations.

Chile: Pinochet and the Military Coup

- **1973 Coup:** The coup led by General Augusto Pinochet, which overthrew the democratically elected government of Salvador Allende, was backed financially and logistically by the U.S.
- **Consequences:** Under Pinochet's regime, Chile endured years of brutal repression, torture, and assassinations. U.S. support aimed to ensure a regime aligned with free-market policies and capitalism.

Argentina and the Military Dictatorship

- During Argentina's military dictatorship (1976–1983), the U.S. provided political and material support to consolidate its interests in the region.
- The regime's brutal repression led to thousands of disappearances and deaths, while American economic and strategic interests remained secure.

5. The Role of Secret Agencies and Military Training

CIA and Military Training

- The Central Intelligence Agency (CIA) played a crucial role in training and supporting Latin American armed forces.
- Many military leaders were trained in the U.S. and sent back to their countries to establish authoritarian regimes and suppress political opposition.

School of the Americas

- The School of the Americas, located in Panama, trained hundreds of military officers from various Latin American countries, becoming a symbol of U.S. interventions.
- Many of these officers were directly involved in human rights violations and political repression in their home countries.

6. Social and Political Impact

Repression and Social Inequality

- The establishment of these dictatorships often led to impoverishment, land expropriation, and social inequality, with workers and peasants being the most affected.
- Natural resources were frequently exploited by American companies, leaving local populations in extreme poverty and economic dependence.

Corruption and Social Unrest

- In many countries, corruption and incompetence in U.S.-backed governments created cycles of social and political unrest, resulting in protests, riots, and, in some cases, civil war.

7. The Decline of Direct Interventions

In the current context, the U.S. maintains a presence in Latin America, but its approach has shifted:

- **Soft Power:** Rather than direct military interventions, the U.S. prefers using soft power through economic aid and trade agreements.
- **Diplomatic Initiatives:** Efforts are now focused on NGOs, trade deals, and investments, though the intent to maintain control and influence over the region's economy and politics remains evident.

8. Conclusion

U.S. military interventions and support for dictatorships in Latin America reveal the dark side of American strategies. Despite economic and political justifications, the reality is that the U.S. often prioritized its own interests, sacrificing the well-being of local populations and disregarding human rights.

The relationship between the U.S. and Latin America is a crucial chapter for understanding the impact of American political decisions on the economic, social, and cultural contexts of the region. It demonstrates how the pursuit of power and influence has come at a high cost, marked by exploitation, repression, and often the suffering of the people living in Latin American countries.

CHAPTER 7: BRAZIL AND THE USA – A RELATIONSHIP MARKED BY CONTROL AND CONTRADICTION

1. The 1964 Coup and the Role of the USA

Historical and Geopolitical Context

During the 1960s, Brazil was one of the primary targets of U.S. geopolitical interests in Latin America. In the context of the Cold War, the USA feared the spread of communist ideas and sought to suppress any leftist movements in the region. This placed Brazil in a strategic position, seen as a key point to contain Soviet influence in Latin America.

- **The 1964 Military Coup:** The coup that overthrew João Goulart's government and established a military regime in Brazil had both explicit and covert support from the USA. Declassified documents over the years revealed the role of American agencies, especially the CIA, in training and supporting Brazilian military forces.

- **Objective:** To ensure Brazil remained a capitalist ally and a stronghold of U.S. economic and political influence in Latin America, facilitating trade agreements and strategic investments.

Financial and Logistical Aid

- **Funding and Training:** During the 1960s and 70s, the USA sent financial resources and military training to strengthen the Brazilian armed forces.

- **Political Influence:** American support helped establish the political structure of the military regime, which lasted 21 years and resulted in brutal repression, censorship, torture, and forced exiles of political opponents.

2. BRAZIL AS AN AMERICAN BACKYARD – ECONOMIC RELATIONSHIP AND CULTURAL INFLUENCE

Economic Partnerships and Multinational Dominance

- Brazil is one of the USA's largest economic partners in Latin America, but this relationship has led to economic inequality and dependency.
- Many American companies control key sectors of the Brazilian economy, such as mining, energy, and agribusiness, exploiting natural resources and leaving little room for domestic economic development.

Cultural and Ideological Influence

- American culture dominates Brazilian daily life, from pop music to advertising and cinema.
- Hollywood films, series, and songs are widely consumed in Brazil, creating an *"American Way of Life"* that attracts many young people and social influences.
- Many Brazilians idolize the American dream, believing that life in the USA represents success, freedom, and power.

3. BRAZILIAN IMMIGRANTS IN THE USA – DREAM AND DISILLUSIONMENT

The Pursuit of the Future

- Thousands of Brazilians leave their country seeking a better life in the USA, attracted by promises of opportunities, jobs, and economic success.
- The presence of Brazilians in states like Massachusetts, Florida, and New Jersey demonstrates the strong connection between the two nations.

Obstacles and American Disdain

- Despite this close relationship, Brazilians often face prejudice, discrimination, and bureaucratic barriers in the USA.
- Many struggle to access the job market, accept lower wages, and deal with documentation and the American immigration system.
- **Entry Restrictions and Persecution:** The American bureaucracy and strict immigration policies make obtaining a visa and permanent residency difficult, reflecting the USA's disregard for Brazilian immigrants.

4. STRATEGIC COOPERATION AND DEPENDENCY

Military Partnerships and Training

- Like the 1964 coup, the USA continues to have a significant influence on the training of Brazilian armed forces.

- Joint military exercises and training programs continue to strengthen ties between the military forces of the two countries, serving both American interests and the Brazilian government's aim to maintain political and economic alignment with the USA.

Trade Agreements and Investments

- Various agreements between the USA and Brazil aim to strengthen bilateral trade, but many are disproportionate and favor American interests.

- Large American multinational companies dominate Brazil's internal market, ensuring substantial profits, while Brazil remains dependent on these companies, losing control over its own resources.

5. THE CONTRADICTION OF THE AMERICAN DREAM AND REAL DISDAIN

Aspiration and Reality

- Many Brazilians still dream of living in the USA, believing they will find success and stability there.

- However, reports of racial discrimination, economic hardships, and immigration barriers reveal the harsh reality many face when attempting to live this dream.

- American culture is sold as an ideal but rarely considers the challenges and obstacles Brazilians must overcome to achieve this goal.

Lack of Support and Solidarity

- Despite significant investments and agreements between the two countries, the USA rarely supports Brazil on social and political issues.

- Problems like urban violence, social inequality, and corruption do not receive substantial American attention, highlighting the limited interest of the USA in addressing Brazil's internal issues.

6. CONCLUSION

The relationship between the USA and Brazil is marked by strategic, economic, and political interests, but also by disdain, control, and inequality.

- In pursuing economic influence and regional power, the USA has used Brazil as a testing ground for power strategies, both through support of military coups and through multinational investments and trade.
- The relationship also presents a paradoxical scenario: Brazilians dream of migrating to the USA, attracted by the American ideal, but often encounter racial, social, and bureaucratic barriers.

This relationship symbolizes the American imperialist dynamic, where corporate interests and state power often take precedence over social well-being and the dignity of local populations. Brazil, as a strategic partner, continues to be a nation where the relationship with the USA brings significant external gains but deep internal and systemic losses.

CHAPTER 8: CASES OF ESPIONAGE AND SABOTAGE OF DEMOCRACIES – THE EMPIRE OF SHADOWS

1. The Systemic Practice of U.S. Espionage

The United States not only maintains economic and political relations with the world but also plays a crucial role in global espionage, often violating the sovereignty of other nations. From agencies like the CIA, NSA, and FBI, American espionage is a fundamental pillar of international strategies, aiming to protect economic and political interests, manipulate scenarios, and weaken potential adversaries.

The Purposes of Espionage

- **Political Control:** The main objective is to influence political decisions in foreign countries, ensuring governments that align ideologically and economically with U.S. interests.

- **Economic Control:** American companies often have access to privileged information that aids in strategic investments and financial decisions.

- **National Security and Military Domination:** Espionage also seeks to anticipate military movements and gain strategic advantages on the battlefield.

2. THE CIA AND THE SUBVERSION OF DEMOCRACIES

Interventionism in Latin America

The CIA played a central role in sabotaging and overthrowing democracies across Latin America. Various coups and clandestine operations were carried out to protect American interests and combat communism, resulting in severe social and political consequences for the affected countries.

Chile Coup (1973)

- The coup that overthrew Salvador Allende's socialist government in Chile is one of the most well-known examples.

- The CIA financed and supported secret operations that facilitated the coup led by General Augusto Pinochet, replacing a democratically elected government with a brutal military regime.

- This ensured American economic interests in the country, consolidating the presence of multinational corporations in control of Chile's wealth, such as mining and agriculture.

Guatemala (1954)

- Another iconic case is **Operation PBSUCCESS** in Guatemala, where the CIA orchestrated the downfall of the democratically elected government of Jacobo Árbenz in 1954.

- Árbenz implemented land reform policies that affected the interests of **United Fruit Company**, a powerful American company.

- The result was the establishment of a military dictatorship that lasted for years, leaving Guatemalan society in suffering and social instability.

Iran Sabotage – Operation Ajax (1953)

- In Iran, the CIA helped organize the coup known as **"Operation Ajax"** in 1953 to overthrow Prime Minister Mohammed Mossadegh, who had nationalized the country's oil industry.

- Mossadegh was seen as a threat to American and British oil company interests.

- The coup allowed the CIA and **BP** to maintain control over Iranian oil reserves, ensuring profitable exploitation of these resources for the U.S. and its allies.

3. THE SNOWDEN CASE – TRUTH EXPOSED

Edward Snowden and the Revelation of Secrets

In 2013, former NSA agent **Edward Snowden** exposed the scale of U.S. espionage operations to the world. He brought to light clandestine and illegal practices that demonstrated how the U.S. monitors not only political enemies but also close allies.

- **Monitoring World Leaders:** Snowden revealed that the NSA was conducting large-scale espionage against foreign leaders, including **Angela Merkel**, the then-Chancellor of Germany.

- **Mass Privacy Violations:** The revelations also exposed the extent of NSA monitoring of American citizens and individuals around the world.

4. ESPIONAGE AND SABOTAGE IN EUROPE – THE SKRIPAL CASE AND HIDDEN INFLUENCE

The Skripal Case and U.S. Agencies' Role

- Russia, as a long-standing adversary of the U.S., became a constant target for American espionage operations.

- The case of **Sergei Skripal**, a former Russian spy, exemplifies sabotage and espionage where the CIA and American allies seek to destabilize operations and secure control over information and influence.

5. MANIPULATION AND INFLUENCE IN THE GLOBAL FINANCIAL SYSTEM

Wall Street and the American Financial Conspiracy

- Many American intelligence agencies focus on manipulating the global financial system to benefit American companies and economic power.

- With secret strategies, the U.S. dollar is used as a tool for financial control, turning the U.S. into the epicenter of global economic decision-making.

- Financial manipulations in European and Asian markets show how the dollar serves as both a power instrument and a means of enriching American elites.

6. SOCIAL AND ETHICAL IMPACT – THE DESTRUCTION OF DEMOCRACIES

Losses in Democratic Societies

- American interventions in democracies often result in social disintegration, poverty, and political repression.

- These countries not only lose their sovereignty but also their ability to make democratic and autonomous decisions, with American multinational corporations and external financial institutions taking control of local economies.

Lack of Transparency

- The secrecy of operations conducted by the CIA and modern intelligence agencies keeps citizens and even allies in the dark.

- Many nations struggle to regain social and economic stability after American operations, leaving a legacy of instability and underdevelopment.

7. CONCLUSION

The United States not only plays a central role on the global stage as an economic and military powerhouse but also implements clandestine practices that destroy democracies, violate national sovereignty, and exploit resources and interests at the expense of local populations.

Agencies like the **CIA and NSA** reveal a system where the U.S. uses espionage and sabotage to consolidate power and influence, implementing silent and effective control over governments and resources worldwide. In the name of economic and political power, the U.S. subverts democratic principles, perpetuates inequalities, and exploits both allies and adversaries.

It is a system of power that benefits only the American empire and its financial interests, while the vast majority of people in the affected countries live under the weight of the consequences and destruction caused by American intervention.

CHAPTER 9: THE ILLUSION OF MILITARY POWER – HEROES OR FAILURES?

1. Media and the Marketing of American Might

The United States often presents itself as the world's greatest military force – a power that brings stability to the world and defends democratic values. However, reality diverges significantly from the image projected by media and propaganda. The true military history of the U.S. is far from the glorious victories and heroic accomplishments often showcased in movies and advertising campaigns. Instead, the U.S. has a history marked by failures, humiliating defeats, and questionable decisions, revealing the fragility of its military might.

2. THE ATOMIC BOMB AND THE ILLUSION OF MILITARY POWER

Hiroshima and Nagasaki – A Cruel and Disproportionate Display of Power

It is undeniable that the only truly impactful "achievement" of the U.S. in World War II was the decision to drop two atomic bombs in Hiroshima and Nagasaki. However, this does not represent a legitimate act of military prowess; rather, it was a brutal act that highlighted the destructive capacity of atomic bombs rather than direct combat strength.

- **Propaganda and Intimidation:** Dropping these bombs was both a test of technological capabilities and a message to the Soviets at the beginning of the Cold War.

- **Lack of Real Military Glory:** U.S. power did not emerge from prolonged battles and sophisticated military strategies but rather from the devastating and ruthless use of this new technology.

3. THE VIETNAM FAILURE – THE HUMILIATION OF AN EMPIRE

The Vietnam War – Defeat on Foreign Soil

The Vietnam War is one of the most emblematic chapters of this failure. The United States, with its technical and military superiority, was defeated by Vietnamese guerrillas who used guerrilla tactics and local knowledge.

- **Unprepared Troops and a Failed Strategy:** Despite a colossal military investment and the deployment of hundreds of thousands of soldiers, the U.S. failed to overcome Vietnamese resistance.

- **Internal Impact:** This defeat not only weakened American military power but also had profound social impacts, such as the decline in soldier morale and an increase in psychological and social trauma among the American population.

4. OTHER FAILED WARS AND COUPS

Iraq War – Lies and Disasters

In 2003, the United States invaded Iraq, claiming the search for weapons of mass destruction – a justification that later proved baseless and fabricated.

- **Defeats and Instability:** The invasion resulted in a prolonged war with no decisive victory and the destruction of the country, failing to deliver the promised "freedom."
- **Social and Regional Chaos:** Instead, Iraq plunged into a scenario of violence, with extremist groups like ISIS gaining power and destabilizing the entire region.

Afghanistan – Two Decades of Failure

The invasion of Afghanistan, which began in 2001, also highlighted the failure of American military power:

- **Two Decades, No Victory:** Despite promises of victory and control over the country, the U.S. withdrew in August 2021, defeated, leaving power in the hands of the Taliban.
- **Billion-Dollar Investment, Disastrous Outcome:** Trillions of dollars were spent, and thousands of American lives were lost, but the final outcome was the absolute control of the Taliban, showcasing how the U.S. failed to establish a lasting and efficient military presence in Afghanistan.

North Korea – The Military Stalemate

Another significant example of U.S. failure in prolonged conflicts is the Korean War:

- **A Lasting Stalemate:** Despite a robust military presence and advanced technology, the U.S. failed to achieve victory on Korean soil, resulting only in the 1953 armistice, without a definitive resolution.

- **Permanent Division:** This left North and South Korea permanently divided, reflecting the American military and strategic stalemate.

5. ESPIONAGE AND SABOTAGE – HIDDEN STRENGTH AND UNDERGROUND STRATEGIES

CIA and Sabotage

The U.S. frequently relies on clandestine agencies, like the CIA, to conduct secret operations where direct military force is replaced by espionage and sabotage.

- **Middle Eastern and Latin American Coups:** Many of these operations, which include overthrowing governments, supporting dictatorships, and clandestine funding, reveal the real weakness of American military power, replaced by manipulation and financial influence.

- **Reliance on Unconventional Tactics:** This demonstrates that U.S. power does not stem from superior military skills but from economic and subversive strategies, like espionage, manipulation, and indirect funding.

6. U.S. MILITARY OWNERSHIP AND THE MARKETING OF POWER

Excessive Propaganda and an Unarmed Reality

The U.S. uses its media power to create an impressive marketing narrative about its military strength:

- **Movies and News Outlets:** Hollywood and American media often portray the American soldier as an invincible hero, but real military facts show a much weaker and more problematic scenario.

- **Disproportionate Investments:** Spending trillions on military technology and equipment does not equate to real battle power. Often, investments are mere marketing and propaganda expenses rather than effective strategic actions.

7. CONCLUSION – THE TRUE FACE OF THE U.S. AS A MILITARY POWER

The idea of the United States as the world's greatest military force is, at best, a myth built on a combination of media propaganda and economic interests. Historically, the U.S. lacks a significant number of relevant military victories but instead has a long history of defeats, stalemates, and failures.

American power is more evident in its espionage agencies, economic influence, and political and financial manipulation strategies than in glorious battles or conventional military victories. The true face of the U.S., therefore, is not that of an invincible and heroic force but of a system where military strength is often replaced by economic influence, subversion, and manipulation.

CHAPTER 10: THE WATERGATE CASE – POLITICAL ESPIONAGE AND THE COLLAPSE OF POWER

1. The Beginning of the Watergate Case – Espionage and Ambition

On June 17, 1972, American history was marked by one of its greatest political scandals: the Watergate Case. The scandal's name comes from the Watergate building in Washington D.C., which housed the Democratic National Committee's offices. This case exposed the dark side of American political power, corruption at high levels, and the fragility of the nation's democratic structures.

At the time, President Richard Nixon, a leader of the Republican Party, sought re-election in 1972 and implemented espionage strategies against the Democratic Party. However, this obsessive pursuit of power ended up exposing what many had already suspected: corruption and questionable methods within the American government.

2. THE SCANDAL AND THE ARREST OF THE INTRUDERS

The pivotal point of the case occurred when five men were arrested while attempting to break into the Democratic National Committee's headquarters located in the Watergate building. Their mission was to spy on documents and install listening devices, but this operation ended up uncovering a much larger plot than a simple act of espionage.

- **High-Level Orders:** Investigations revealed that the scheme was orchestrated by the presidential office and figures close to Nixon.

- **Primary Objective:** Spy on and sabotage the Democratic Party to gain electoral advantages, exposing the use of illegal and unethical practices at the heart of American political power.

3. THE MEDIA'S ROLE AND THE INFLUENCE OF THE PRESS

Bob Woodward and Carl Bernstein

The Watergate case was extensively investigated and exposed by the American media, mainly by Washington Post journalists Bob Woodward and Carl Bernstein. They played a crucial role in revealing the scandal's details, connecting espionage activities to Nixon's cabinet members.

- **Media Impact:** Their work illustrated the power of American journalism as a watchdog of the government, a force capable of challenging even the president.

- **Independent Investigation:** The courage and determination of the journalists in seeking the truth contrasted with the government's desire to conceal corruption, symbolizing the struggle between established powers and those committed to uncovering the truth.

4. NIXON'S RESIGNATION – AN HUMILIATING OUTCOME

On August 9, 1974, Richard Nixon resigned as President of the United States, becoming the only president in American history to do so.

Congressional Pressure and the Power of Impeachment

- **Impeachment Imminent:** The evidence against Nixon was so clear and extensive that Congress considered impeachment, which would leave the president in an untenable position.

- **Resignation as Salvation:** Resigning was the only way to avoid impeachment, maintaining some institutional dignity and preventing the country from descending into political chaos.

5. IMPLICATIONS OF THE WATERGATE CASE – DEMOCRATIC CHALLENGES AND LOSS OF TRUST

Public Disillusionment

The Watergate case not only tarnished the presidential image but also had deep implications for American public trust in the government.

- **Widespread Distrust:** The revelation of espionage and illegal activities by high-level government figures made Americans question the legitimacy of government institutions, increasing skepticism and political alienation.

- **Trust Crisis:** Confidence in politicians, congress members, and public institutions was severely undermined, resulting in a state of disillusionment that persists in the collective imagination to this day.

Government Changes and Political Reforms

In response to the Watergate case, several institutional and legislative changes were implemented:

1. **The Ethics in Government Act:** Established strict transparency and ethical measures for government members.

2. **Strengthening Congressional Oversight:** Made the legislative branch a more active watchdog of executive actions, ensuring a greater balance of power among branches of government.

3. **Media and Investigation Reorganization:** Emphasized the importance of an independent media as a crucial element in democracy, ensuring journalists maintained their role as political

watchdogs.

6. THE WATERGATE CASE AND AMERICAN POWER – A CRITICAL REFLECTION

The Hidden Face of American "Democracy"

- **Government Espionage:** The case exposed how high-ranking officials used illegal practices to maintain power and influence political landscapes.
- **Worn Institutions and Hidden Powers:** Highlighted the influence of secret agencies, like the CIA, and how the government could operate clandestinely, betraying public trust.

Questioning Patriotism and Political Motivations

- **Propaganda vs. Reality:** The U.S. often presents itself as a defender of human rights and promoter of democracy, but cases like Watergate reveal a reality where power is exercised unethically and manipulatively, focused solely on political survival and success.
- **Power and Responsibility:** The case questions the leaders' responsibility to the people and democracy, exposing the ethical dilemmas and mistakes of absolute power.

7. CONCLUSION

The Watergate case not only brought down Nixon's government but also unveiled the true operation of American institutions and the methods through which power is exercised in the United States. More than a case of political espionage and presidential defeat, it serves as a warning that the facade of democracy and ethics often hides authoritarian practices and corruption.

The image of the United States as a symbol of democracy and moral strength was severely weakened, highlighting a landscape of political manipulation, clandestine espionage, and self-serving interests – a stark contrast between public rhetoric and the reality of American governmental power.

CHAPTER 11: THE 2008 ECONOMIC CRISIS – SAVING THE RICH, CRUSHING THE POOR

1. The Pre-Crisis Scenario – The Easy Credit Party and Financial Out-of-Control

Before 2008, the American economy experienced a period of euphoria, marked by rapid growth and apparent financial stability. The dream of home ownership, easy credit, and a constant consumer-driven lifestyle seemed within everyone's reach. However, behind this facade, the United States was laying the foundation for what would become the worst economic crisis since the Great Depression of 1929.

The Role of Banks and the Financial System

Uncontrolled Credit and Subprime Mortgages:

At the heart of the crisis was the subprime mortgage market – loans given to individuals with unstable financial histories. Banks offered these mortgages without properly verifying the borrowers' ability to repay their debts.

- Many Americans, lured by the dream of home ownership, took out mortgages they knew they couldn't afford.
- Financial institutions, seeking quick profits, began bundling these mortgages into complex financial products known as *derivatives*, and selling them on the global market.

The Collapse of Lehman Brothers

In September 2008, the collapse of Lehman Brothers, a cornerstone of the American financial market, became the symbol of the financial meltdown.

- The bankruptcy of this bank triggered a domino effect, affecting the entire U.S. financial system and spreading globally, leading to a worldwide recession.

- The U.S. government's decision to let Lehman Brothers fail without a bailout demonstrated the major financial institutions' disregard for ordinary citizens and their prioritization of corporate profits.

2. THE ROLE OF THE GOVERNMENT AND THE LACK OF REGULATION

George W. Bush and the Deregulation Act

The crisis scenario was worsened by the U.S. government's approach to financial market deregulation:

- During George W. Bush's administration, there was a significant push for deregulating financial institutions to stimulate economic growth and business freedom.
- The lack of oversight on banks and financial companies' practices allowed risky and speculative financial products to emerge, creating an unstable and unpredictable market.

The Role of the Federal Reserve

The Federal Reserve (the U.S. Central Bank) also played a significant role in the crisis:

- For years, the Federal Reserve maintained extremely low interest rates, encouraging easy credit and excessive consumer spending.
- Instead of properly regulating the market, central banks often allowed the financial sector to pursue its interests, even if it meant jeopardizing the country's economic stability.

3. RESCUING THE RICH – SAVING THE FINANCIAL SYSTEM, IGNORING THE PEOPLE

The $700 Billion Bailout Plan (TARP)

When the crisis reached its peak, the U.S. government, under President George W. Bush, implemented the famous *Troubled Asset Relief Program* (TARP):

- **Bailing Out Banks:** TARP injected $700 billion into banks and large financial institutions, ensuring their survival and stability.

- **Little Protection for the Common Citizen:** Although the banks were saved, workers and ordinary families were left on the sidelines. Many lost their homes, jobs, and savings.

The Role of Wall Street

Large financial companies and executives on Wall Street continued to live in luxury:

- **Million-Dollar Bonuses:** Despite the financial rescue, many banking executives received multimillion-dollar bonuses, ignoring the high unemployment rates and the suffering of American families.

- **Preserving Fortunes:** The crisis revealed how public money was used to save elite interests without distributing resources or benefits to those who actually sustain the economy.

4. HOW THE POOR AND MIDDLE CLASS WERE AFFECTED

Loss of Homes and the Collapsed Real Estate Market

- Many American families lost their homes due to mortgage defaults, a direct result of financial institutions' predatory practices.
- The real estate market collapse left millions of Americans deeply in debt and without the necessary economic support, exacerbating poverty and insecurity.

Mass Unemployment and Social Instability

- The economic collapse resulted in an alarming unemployment rate, reaching levels of over 10% in the years following the 2008 collapse.
- The American middle class was the hardest hit, losing savings, investments, and economic stability.

Social Assistance and the Failure of Public Policies

- Many people depended on social programs and government assistance, but public policy responses were slow and ineffective.
- Social policies and assistance programs failed to address the scale of the problems, leaving many citizens facing hunger, homelessness, and a lack of access to healthcare services.

5. LESSONS THE U.S. LEFT BEHIND – THE RESPONSIBILITY OF THE CAPITALIST SYSTEM

The Nature of the Capitalist System and Inequality

- The 2008 crisis highlighted the functioning of the American capitalist system and its relationship with social inequality.
- American capitalism often requires economic inequality since corporate profits rely on disparities between rich and poor.

Deregulation Policies and the Cost of Profit

- The ideology of minimal government intervention and relentless pursuit of profit ultimately cost the financial and social system's stability.
- This demonstrates how capitalism can be a system that benefits only the powerful while neglecting those who sustain the economy through work and effort.

6. CONCLUSION

The 2008 economic crisis not only shook the financial landscape of the United States but also exposed the true nature of the country's policies and practices. The bailout of large corporations at the expense of ordinary families revealed the fragility of the promises of the *American Dream*, where stability and prosperity depend solely on luck and the decisions of financial elites.

The 2008 case serves as a warning about the urgent need for financial and regulatory reforms, highlighting that American prosperity is often not for everyone. The American system, in its relentless pursuit of profit and market freedom, left a legacy of social inequality, poverty, and lost hope for millions of citizens.

CHAPTER 12: THE CIA AND SECRET OPERATIONS – POWER, MANIPULATION, AND TORTURE

1. The CIA – An Instrument of American Domination

The Central Intelligence Agency (CIA) is not just an intelligence force, but one of the most emblematic elements of secret operations and American power. Since its founding in 1947, the CIA has been responsible for covert operations that extend beyond intelligence gathering, involving political manipulation, subversion, and control, both domestically and internationally.

Many critics view the CIA as one of the prime examples of American imperial operations, highlighting the willingness of the U.S. government to use secret interventions to advance its interests while disregarding human and social consequences.

2. REGIME CHANGES – AMERICAN INTERVENTION IN OTHER NATIONS

One of the most well-known examples of CIA covert operations occurred in 1953, when the agency actively participated in the coup that overthrew Iran's Prime Minister, Mohammad Mossadegh.

- **Mossadegh had nationalized the oil industry**, which threatened the interests of major American and British oil companies.
- The CIA, in collaboration with British intelligence, orchestrated **Operation Ajax**, which led to Mossadegh's removal and bolstered the power of Shah Mohammad Reza Pahlavi, a U.S. ally in the Middle East.
- This intervention not only consolidated U.S. economic control over Iranian oil but also resulted in years of social repression and instability, alongside human and political damage to the nation.

Guatemala – The 1954 Coup

Another significant case is the 1954 coup in Guatemala, where the CIA assisted in overthrowing the government of **Jacobo Árbenz**, then the president of the country.

- **Árbenz sought to implement agrarian reforms**, which negatively impacted the interests of the United Fruit Company, which owned large amounts of land in Guatemala.
- The CIA, aiming to protect these corporate interests, executed **Operation PBSUCCESS**, which involved destabilization, guerrilla warfare, and violence across the nation.
- This coup not only removed Árbenz from power but also left Guatemala in decades of internal conflicts and instability, marked by violence and political repression.

3. MKULTRA – UNETHICAL EXPERIMENTS AND MENTAL TORTURE

Origins of MKUltra

The MKUltra project was one of the most infamous and controversial episodes involving the CIA in the United States. During the Cold War, the CIA sought methods to strengthen American control and influence in psychological warfare and espionage, aiming to gain an advantage over the Soviets and other rival powers.

- **Objective:** To test chemical substances, drugs (mainly LSD), and mind-control techniques on humans.
- Operations included everything from **hypnosis and sensory deprivation to the use of toxic substances**, with the goal of manipulating behaviors and obtaining confidential information.

Human Experiments

- Many victims were **innocent civilians, prisoners, and even government employees**, who were subjected to intensive and dehumanizing physical and psychological treatments.
- Survivors often suffered **irreversible brain damage, mental health issues, memory loss, and profound psychological trauma**.

Ethical and Social Implications

- MKUltra raises questions about the true role of American intelligence agencies and their willingness to use brutal and unethical methods in the name of national interest.
- After years of secrecy, many of these experiments came to light in the late 1970s, leading to **scandals and a loss of credibility for the CIA and the American government** among the public and society.

4. THE CIA AND THE VIETNAM WAR – TORTURE AND MANIPULATION

Use of Agent Orange and Torture

During the Vietnam War, the CIA implemented secret operations and brutal experiments that caused immeasurable harm to both Vietnamese people and American soldiers.

- **Agent Orange:**
    - A chemical substance used by Americans in Vietnam to **eliminate vegetation**, depriving the Viet Cong of natural hiding spots.
    - However, Agent Orange caused **severe and permanent health issues, such as cancer and physical disabilities**, for both American soldiers and Vietnamese civilians.

- **Use of Torture and Psychological Guerrilla Warfare**
    - The CIA carried out **clandestine operations and guerrilla warfare** to destabilize the communist movement in Vietnam.
    - American and Vietnamese soldiers were often subjected to **brutal interrogation sessions, sensory deprivation, and sleep deprivation methods**.

5. THE CIA AND GLOBAL CONTROL – DISHONEST PARTNERSHIPS AND INTERNATIONAL DESTABILIZATION

Alliance with Dictators

- The CIA frequently **supported dictatorial regimes around the world**, from the Middle East to Latin America.
- Dictators who served **U.S. strategic and economic interests** were often backed by the CIA, regardless of significant human rights violations in their countries.

Notable Examples

- **Chile – The 1973 Coup:** The CIA supported the military coup that **overthrew Salvador Allende's government**, facilitating the rise of Augusto Pinochet, whose policies and repression led to years of suffering and torture for the Chilean population.
- **Middle Eastern Operations:** Numerous secret operations were implemented over the decades to **strengthen alliances with Middle Eastern dictators**, aiming to control oil markets and maintain regional influence.

6. CONCLUSION

The CIA represents the dark side of American power – a symbol of secret operations and the manipulation of U.S. interests on a global scale. Whether through interventions to overthrow foreign leaders, unethical human experiments, or support for dictators, the CIA shows that the pursuit of American strategic and economic interests often comes at the expense of **human rights, ethics, and social responsibility**.

This chapter reveals how the United States not only expands its military and economic influence but also operates from the shadows, promoting control, repression, and brutality. In the world of CIA secret operations, the idea of the **"American Dream" shatters**, replaced by a legacy of exploitation, manipulation, and absolute power.

CHAPTER 14: UNMENTIONED SCANDALS AND CORRUPTION

The United States, often portrayed as a symbol of transparency and good governance, also has a history of scandals and corruption that go beyond the episodes already discussed. Many of these lesser-known stories reveal the dark and problematic functioning of American institutions, where the pursuit of power and profit often outweighs ethical principles and social responsibility.

1. THE ENRON CASE – FINANCIAL FRAUD AND CORPORATE COLLAPSE

In the early 2000s, Enron, an American energy giant, became one of the largest examples of financial fraud in U.S. history.

- **Accounting Manipulation:**
    - The company hid billions in debt, using fraudulent accounting methods to inflate profits and conceal losses.
    - When the truth came to light in 2001, Enron declared bankruptcy, leaving thousands of investors and employees without their investments and savings.

- **Social and Ethical Impact:**
    - Many employees lost their savings, retirement funds, and financial stability.
    - The case generated deep distrust in the financial market, highlighting the lack of regulation and ethics among large corporations and investors.

2. THE FAST AND FURIOUS CASE – ARMS TRADE AND GOVERNMENT NEGLIGENCE

In the late 2000s, the Fast and Furious operation, led by the Bureau of Alcohol, Tobacco, Firearms, and Explosives (ATF), revealed issues in arms control between Mexico and the U.S.

- **Poorly Planned Objective:**
    - The operation aimed to track weapons sold in the U.S. that were smuggled into Mexico to identify drug cartels.
    - However, the ATF allowed thousands of weapons to be smuggled into Mexico, many of which were later used in violent crimes among Mexican cartels.

- **Consequences:**
    - The operation's failure resulted in the deaths of several Mexican and American police officers.
    - The incident exposed the negligence of American agencies and the risks of arms control policies, revealing serious flaws in combating international arms trafficking.

3. THE NSA CASE – MASS SURVEILLANCE AND PRIVACY VIOLATIONS

The National Security Agency (NSA) is known for its mass surveillance capabilities, revealed in leaked documents by former agent Edward Snowden in 2013.

- **Global Espionage:**
    - The NSA conducted large-scale monitoring operations, surveilling communications between American and foreign citizens, often violating individual privacy.
    - Documents exposed the NSA's collaboration with major technology companies like Google, Facebook, and Microsoft, facilitating the collection and storage of sensitive information.

- **Ethical and Political Impact:**
    - This case sparked debates about individual freedom, privacy, and civil rights, placing the U.S. in an international position of scrutiny regarding transparency and ethics.
    - Many nations and citizens began questioning the legitimacy of American practices related to privacy rights and freedom of expression.

4. THE WATER POLLUTION CRISIS – FLINT, MICHIGAN

In 2014, the city of Flint, Michigan, faced an environmental public health disaster that drew worldwide attention.

- **Water Contamination:**
    - The local government altered the water supply source, using water from the Flint River, which ultimately became contaminated with dangerous levels of lead.
    - This affected thousands of residents, especially children, who suffered from severe physical and cognitive impacts.

- **Government Responsibility and Failures:**
    - The scandal exposed the failure of government agencies to ensure basic public safety and health.
    - Many families were left homeless and faced financial difficulties in repairing health and property damages.

5. CORPORATE LOBBYING AND POLITICAL INFLUENCE

The U.S. has a system where corporate lobbying significantly impacts political decision-making.

- **Politics and Money:**
    - Companies like Big Pharma, banks, and the defense industry influence laws and government decisions through powerful lobbying groups, guaranteed by campaign funding.
    - This means political decisions are often based on economic interests rather than social welfare or ethical considerations.

- **Favorable Laws and Social Costs:**
    - Critical aspects, such as labor legislation, financial regulations, and health policies, are often shaped to benefit these corporations.
    - This resulted in policies that undervalue workers and neglect access to essential services and healthcare for millions of American citizens.

CONCLUSION

Scandals and corruption reveal that America's image as a symbol of ethics and responsibility is just a facade. Whether through corporate financial fraud, disastrous government policies in environmental and social areas, or the disproportionate influence of corporate lobbying, the truth is that American governance often fails its commitments to the common citizen.

These lesser-known stories show that the U.S. is not only the world's economic and military powerhouse but also a complex system frequently burdened by hidden interests and questionable practices, where the pursuit of power and profit often comes before human rights and social ethics.

ARMS SALES AND SUPPORT FOR GLOBAL CONFLICTS

1. The Global Arms Market: Exportation and Profits

The U.S. is the world's largest arms exporter, and the arms trade is a core part of the Military-Industrial Complex. The country not only sustains its own armed forces but also supplies many countries and groups worldwide.

- **International Market Dominance:**
  - Companies like Lockheed Martin, Raytheon, Boeing, and General Dynamics dominate the American military export landscape.
  - It is estimated that around 70% of global arms exports come from the United States, including combat planes, tanks, pistols, and ammunition.

- **Government Contracts:**
  - The U.S. government makes contracts with these companies, which, in turn, export products to other countries with Congress and the State Department's approval.
  - These contracts ensure a continued financial flow and create jobs in the military sector, while maintaining the economic power of large Military-Industrial Complex companies.

- **Geopolitical Influence:**
  - Arms sales serve as a strategic tool to consolidate political and military alliances with other nations.
  - Many sales agreements include clauses ensuring U.S. control and influence over the politics and internal decisions of these countries.

2. SUPPORT FOR CONFLICTS: STRATEGIC ALLIANCES' IMPORTANCE

The U.S. not only sells weapons but also plays a crucial role in supporting global conflicts through alliances, providing equipment, and offering financial support to armed groups and countries at war.

Middle East

- In the Middle East, the U.S. has provided continuous military support to countries like Saudi Arabia, Israel, and Turkey, becoming a key player in regional dynamics.
- Military sales and financial support ensure these countries maintain their military strength and regional influence.

Africa

- In African conflicts, the U.S. plays a significant role in supplying weapons and direct military support.
- Arms contracts with countries like Somalia and the Democratic Republic of Congo showcase the U.S.'s efforts to expand influence and control over regional resources and political dynamics.

Latin America

- The U.S.'s relationship with Latin America includes massive arms sales, often used to combat guerrilla movements and criminal factions.
- Military contracts in Brazil, Colombia, and other countries aim to fight drug trafficking and instability but often result in criticism for excessive violence and military intervention in communities.

3. ARMS SMUGGLING AND FUNDING ARMED GROUPS

Besides official sales, the United States is also involved in arms smuggling and funding armed groups worldwide.

- **Smuggling and Informal Trade:**
  - There is evidence that the U.S. facilitates the clandestine shipment of arms to militant groups in conflict zones, both in the Middle East and Latin America.
  - This happens through CIA operations and other intelligence services, where clandestine equipment supply is used to strengthen allies and destabilize adversaries.

- **Insurgent and Guerrilla Groups:**
  - Often, these weapons and supplies end up in insurgent factions and guerrilla groups, financed or supported by American strategic interests.
  - Funding these groups aims to fight political enemies and push U.S. geopolitical agendas.

CONCLUSION

The United States' role in supporting global conflicts and indiscriminate arms sales reveals the true agenda of the Military-Industrial Complex, which seeks profit and power at the expense of peace and national stability. War, in many cases, is not about defending democracy or freedom but rather an economic machine that generates wealth for private companies and powerful political interests while destabilizing communities and draining national resources worldwide.

This scenario challenges the official narrative of the U.S. as global defenders of justice and freedom, exposing the real motives behind political decisions and financial and military support, making it clear that, for the government and its companies, war is an investment—not a sacrifice.

CHAPTER 15: THE DESTRUCTION OF INDIGENOUS PEOPLES

1. Genocide and Forced Displacements

Since the arrival of European colonizers, Indigenous peoples in the Americas have faced a brutal process of genocide and forced displacement, which intensified with the founding and expansion of the United States.

- **The Context of Colonization:**
  - It is estimated that the Indigenous population in what would become the United States was around 10 million before the arrival of Europeans. This number declined to fewer than 300,000 by the 19th century due to wars, diseases, and deliberate massacres.
  - The introduction of diseases such as smallpox, typhus, and measles was one of the main causes of mortality. Many of these outbreaks were used as undeclared biological weapons, with reports of deliberately distributing blankets infected with smallpox.

- **War and Territorial Conquest:**
  - The advance of American colonizers and the government forced many tribes to leave their ancestral lands. Between 1830 and 1850, the Indian Removal Policy led to the infamous Trail of Tears, where tens of thousands of Cherokee, Choctaw, Creek, Seminole, and other tribes were forced to march westward.
  - During these marches, over 4,000 Cherokee died from hunger, diseases, and harsh conditions.

- **Massacres:**
  - Indigenous population massacres occurred on multiple occasions, including the **Sand Creek**

Massacre (1864), where approximately 230 Indigenous people, most women and children, were killed by the American army.

- Another example is the **Wounded Knee Massacre** (1890), where over 300 Lakota Sioux were killed while attempting to surrender.

2. BROKEN PROMISES: TREATIES AND EXPLOITATION

The relationship between the American government and Indigenous tribes was marked by systematic betrayals through fraudulent treaties and unfulfilled promises.

- **Violated Treaties:**
    - Throughout the 19th century, over 370 treaties were signed between the U.S. and Indigenous tribes. Most were later violated or ignored.
    - These treaties often promised land, resources, and protection in exchange for territorial concessions from Indigenous peoples, but the country's expansion and pursuit of wealth frequently took precedence over the promises made.
- **Natural Resource Theft:**
    - When natural resources, such as gold or oil, were discovered on Indigenous lands, tribes were expelled or forcibly dispossessed of their territories.
    - The discovery of gold in the **Black Hills**, sacred land for the Lakota, led to the violation of the **Fort Laramie Treaty** (1868) and the deployment of the army to remove the Lakota from the area.

3. MARGINALIZATION AND CURRENT CONDITIONS

Even after physical and cultural genocide, Indigenous peoples continue to face extreme marginalization and inhumane living conditions.

- **Indian Reservations:**
    - Today, many tribes live on reservations created by the government, which are often located on barren land unsuitable for farming or adequate housing.
    - Living conditions on these reservations are frequently compared to those in countries experiencing extreme poverty. In some communities, life expectancy is 20 years lower than the national average.
- **Poverty and Unemployment:**
    - Around 25% of Indigenous people live below the poverty line, and unemployment rates in some reservations can reach up to 80%.
    - The lack of economic opportunities and government neglect perpetuate a cycle of structural poverty.
- **Violence and Abuse:**
    - Indigenous women face alarmingly high rates of violence and disappearances. According to the FBI, one in three Indigenous women will be raped at some point in their lives, with most perpetrators being non-Indigenous individuals.
    - The crisis of missing Indigenous women, especially in Canada and the U.S., reflects the lack of protection and respect for these communities.

4. RESISTANCE AND RESILIENCE

Despite centuries of oppression, Indigenous peoples continue to resist and fight for their rights.

- **Justice Movements:**
    - The **American Indian Movement (AIM)**, founded in the 1960s, played a crucial role in advocating for Indigenous civil rights. AIM was instrumental in highlighting issues such as tribal sovereignty and violence against Indigenous communities.
    - Protests like **Standing Rock in 2016**, which opposed the construction of the Dakota Access Pipeline, demonstrate the ongoing resistance of Indigenous peoples in defending their rights and sacred lands.
- **Cultural Revitalization:**
    - Despite historical efforts to destroy Indigenous cultures, many tribes have worked to revitalize their languages, traditions, and spirituality.
    - Schools and community programs on various reservations are promoting the teaching of native languages and the practice of traditional ceremonies.

CONCLUSION

The destruction of Indigenous peoples in the United States remains one of the darkest stains on the nation's history. From genocide and forced displacements to ongoing marginalization, the American government has failed to respect Indigenous peoples and their cultures.

As Indigenous peoples continue to fight for justice and equality, their resilience serves as a testament to strength and resistance in the face of centuries of oppression. True reconciliation will only be possible when the United States confronts its history of genocide and marginalization and takes concrete steps to repair the damages caused.

CHAPTER 16: BULLYING CULTURE IN SCHOOLS: AN EPIDEMIC OF CRUELTY

1. The Bullying Phenomenon: An Invisible Epidemic

Bullying in American schools is an endemic problem, fueled by a competitive culture, rigid social hierarchies, and the glorification of aggression in various aspects of American life. Studies show that one in five children in the U.S. is a victim of bullying, whether it be verbal, physical, social, or online.

- **Nature of Bullying:**
  - Bullying often takes subtle and psychological forms, such as social exclusion, but can also escalate into physical assaults or cyberbullying, especially with the growing presence of social media.
  - Stereotypes and prejudices play a significant role: LGBTQIA+ students, Black students, Latinos, and other marginalized groups are often targeted, with devastating consequences.

2. PSYCHOLOGICAL AND SOCIAL IMPACTS

Bullying in schools is not just a childhood problem; it causes deep and lasting impacts that affect victims, aggressors, and even bystanders.

- **Victims:**
    - Children and adolescents who experience bullying face higher rates of anxiety, depression, self-injury, and suicide. Studies show that bullying significantly increases the risk of mental health disorders in adulthood.
    - Academically, victims often underperform because the hostile school environment makes learning unbearable.

- **Aggressors:**
    - Many bullies end up repeating destructive patterns in adulthood, exhibiting criminal or violent behavior.
    - In some cases, childhood bullying is a reflection of abusive or neglectful family environments.

- **Bystanders:**
    - Peers who witness bullying without intervening also face emotional consequences, such as guilt, anxiety, and desensitization to violence.

3. FAMOUS CASES: COLUMBINE AND OTHER SCHOOL SHOOTINGS

The culture of bullying in American schools is often associated with tragic events like mass shootings. One of the most emblematic cases is the Columbine massacre.

- **The Columbine Massacre (1999):**
    - On April 20, 1999, students Eric Harris and Dylan Klebold entered Columbine High School in Colorado armed and killed 13 people, injuring 24 others before taking their own lives.
    - Although motivations have been widely debated, both shooters reported experiencing severe bullying, which fueled their anger and desire for revenge.
    - Columbine became a symbol of the school system's failure and the culture of exclusion and violence in American schools.
- **Other Notable Cases:**
    - **Sandy Hook (2012):** Although not directly linked to bullying, this massacre sparked discussions about mental health and the failure to identify psychological distress in children.
    - **Virginia Tech (2007):** The shooter, Cho Seung-Hui, experienced bullying and social rejection throughout his academic life, which contributed to his isolation and eventual attack.

4. THE ROLE OF SOCIETY AND CULTURE

American culture plays a significant role in perpetuating bullying, whether through toxic masculinity norms, the glorification of winners and losers, or the normalization of violence as a conflict resolution method.

- **Movies and Media:**
    - Popular culture often romanticizes bullying or treats it as a rite of passage, especially in movies and TV shows about American schools.
    - Films like *Mean Girls* and *Carrie* show the devastating impact of bullying but also reflect the trivialization of youthful cruelty.
- **Social Media:**
    - With the rise of social media, bullying has extended beyond school boundaries. Cyberbullying is an extension of traditional bullying, with attacks that can occur 24 hours a day.
    - Platforms like Instagram and TikTok are places where social comparisons, criticism, and public humiliations are frequent.

5. INITIATIVES AND EDUCATIONAL SYSTEM FAILURES

Despite efforts to combat bullying, American schools often fail to protect victims and prevent violence.

- **Anti-Bullying Policies:**
    - Many states have implemented laws requiring schools to adopt anti-bullying policies, but a lack of enforcement and fear of retaliation undermine these measures.
    - Some schools prioritize maintaining a positive public image, often covering up bullying incidents instead of addressing them.
- **Education and Intervention:**
    - Campaigns like *StopBullying.gov* have tried to raise awareness about bullying's impact and promote a culture of empathy.
    - However, without structural changes in how schools handle power dynamics and social exclusion, bullying persists.

CONCLUSION

Bullying in American schools is not just an individual issue but a reflection of broader systemic and cultural failures. A lack of empathy, extreme competitiveness, and the glorification of social hierarchies contribute to this epidemic of cruelty.

School shootings are just the most visible and extreme manifestation of this problem, but the suffering caused by bullying has silent, lifelong repercussions. Addressing this issue requires not only educating children but also transforming society and its cultural priorities, fostering a culture of respect and inclusion.

CHAPTER 17: THE HUMILIATION OF IMMIGRANTS

1. The Land of Opportunities or Exclusion?

The United States is often portrayed as the land of opportunity, but for many immigrants, this vision is cruelly dismantled once they cross the border. From brutal deportations to inhumane conditions in detention centers, the U.S. has a long history of hostility towards those seeking a better future within its borders.

Anti-immigrant rhetoric, fueled by political discourse and social prejudices, paints immigrants as economic, criminal, and cultural threats, creating an environment where humiliation and marginalization are not only common but systematic.

2. BRUTAL DEPORTATIONS AND INHUMANE DETENTION CENTERS

Family Separation Policy:

- During Donald Trump's presidency, the zero-tolerance policy resulted in the separation of thousands of children from their families at the border. Minors were held in detention centers described as "cages," where they faced unsanitary conditions, lack of medical care, and psychological trauma.

- A 2021 report revealed that many children still hadn't been reunited with their families, exposing the administration's negligence and lack of planning.

Detention Centers:

- Human rights organizations describe immigrant detention centers as overcrowded, unsanitary, and dangerous.

- Cases of physical and psychological abuse by staff members are common, and many detainees reported a lack of adequate food, basic hygiene, and access to medical care.

- A notable accusation involved forced sterilizations of detained women, an act echoing eugenic practices historically used to control marginalized populations.

Violent Deportations:

- Deportations carried out hastily and brutally often leave immigrants in extreme vulnerability. Many are sent back to countries facing violence, extreme poverty, or natural disasters, without any consideration for their personal circumstances.

3. PSYCHOLOGICAL IMPACT ON FAMILIES AND COMMUNITIES

U.S. immigration policies have devastating effects on families and communities, both for those living in the U.S. and for the deported.

Childhood Trauma:

- Children separated from their parents at the border experience post-traumatic stress disorder (PTSD), along with emotional and behavioral development issues.
- The constant fear of deportation among families that remain in the U.S. causes anxiety and prevents children from having a normal school and social life.

Family Disintegration:

- The deportation of a family member, often the primary provider, disrupts entire families.
- Wives, children, and relatives who remain in the U.S. face financial difficulties and a profound sense of loss, while deported individuals often live in isolation in their countries of origin, without the means to start over.

Marginalized Communities:

- Immigrant communities suffer from stigma and persecution, exacerbating social and economic inequality.
- The constant threat of deportation also hinders the formation of support networks and civic engagement.

4. RACISM AND XENOPHOBIA: AN EMBEDDED HISTORY

The humiliation of immigrants is not only about contemporary policies but also reflects deeply embedded historical prejudices in American society.

Primary Targets:

- Latino immigrants, particularly Mexicans, are often depicted as "invaders" or "criminals," fueling harsh border policies and hostile attitudes.

- Muslims and Middle Eastern immigrants also faced severe discrimination after the 9/11 attacks, with laws like the Patriot Act enabling surveillance and arbitrary detention of individuals from these groups.

The American Dream Myth:

- While many immigrants risk their lives to pursue the so-called "American Dream," the reality they encounter often involves labor exploitation, discrimination, and the constant fear of deportation.

- Undocumented workers frequently face low wages and dangerous working conditions, without access to basic rights or legal protection.

5. THE TREATMENT OF BRAZILIANS IN THE U.S.

Although Brazilians constitute a significant portion of immigrants in the U.S., their experience reflects a mix of hope and humiliation.

Stereotypes and Devaluation:

- Brazilians often face prejudices based on cultural stereotypes, being treated as inferior or exploited in low-paying jobs.
- Even with academic qualifications, many end up in underpaid jobs due to difficulties in credential validation and language barriers.

Difficult Entry Requirements:

- Despite many Brazilians dreaming of life in the U.S., obtaining a visa is extremely difficult, and cases of Brazilian deportation are frequent.
- The U.S. maintains strict control over Brazilian immigration, often treating them as economic or illegal threats.

Dream or Illusion?

- The reality for Brazilian immigrants contrasts sharply with the idealized image of the U.S. in Brazil, often portrayed in films and TV shows. Many discover that, far from being a "paradise," life in the U.S. can be a nightmare of exploitation, isolation, and prejudice.

6. RESISTANCE AND THE FIGHT FOR JUSTICE

Despite all the challenges, immigrant communities have mobilized to resist humiliation and fight for their rights.

Human Rights Organizations:

- Groups like the ACLU (American Civil Liberties Union) and RAICES provide legal support and fight against inhumane immigration policies.

- These organizations work to expose abuses, offer resources to victims, and push for legislative changes.

Stories of Resilience:

- Many stories of immigrants show that, despite adversity, it is possible to build a new life and resist oppression, shedding light on system failures and inspiring change.

CONCLUSION

The humiliation of immigrants in the U.S. is not only a result of inhumane policies but also of a culture of exclusion and xenophobia deeply rooted in American society. Promises of freedom and opportunity contrast sharply with the reality of exploitation, abuse, and marginalization faced by millions.

For the U.S. to truly become a beacon of hope, it is necessary to address these systemic failures by adopting policies that respect human rights and uphold the dignity of all immigrants, regardless of their origin.

CHAPTER 18: HOSPITAL: PAY OR DIE

1. The American Healthcare System: An Economic Battlefield

In the United States, healthcare is not a right but a luxury. Unlike many developed countries that offer universal healthcare systems, the American model relies on private insurance and a profit-driven hospital system. This creates a cruel reality: those who can pay live; those who can't, die or accumulate unpayable debts.

Hospitals and insurance companies in the U.S. often prioritize profits over care, resulting in millions of people without access to proper treatments. In 2023, over 27 million Americans were uninsured, while many others struggled to afford high premiums and treatments.

2. SYSTEMIC FAILURES: NEGLECT AND EXCLUSION

- **Cost of Treatments:**
    - A simple doctor's visit can cost hundreds of dollars, while hospital stays and surgeries often reach tens or hundreds of thousands of dollars.
    - Essential medications, such as insulin, are sold at exorbitant prices, even when the cost of production is low.
        - For example, the average annual cost for a diabetic can exceed $6,000 just for insulin.
- **Medical Neglect and Systemic Racism:**
    - Studies reveal that racial minorities face disproportionately high rates of medical neglect. Black, Hispanic, and Indigenous patients often receive inferior treatments compared to white patients and suffer from explicit and implicit biases from healthcare professionals.
- **Denial of Treatment:**
    - Uninsured patients are frequently refused or abandoned in hospital corridors, while those with limited insurance face inadequate treatments due to coverage restrictions.

3. DEBT: A SILENT EPIDEMIC

For many Americans, a medical emergency can mean financial ruin.

- **Unpayable Medical Debt:**
  - Over 60% of bankruptcies in the U.S. are directly related to medical debt.
  - A single hospital stay can result in bills exceeding $100,000, especially for critical treatments like cancer care.
- **Eternal Payments:**
  - Indebted families often enter payment plans that last decades, often with high interest, creating a cycle of poverty.
  - Notable cases show people losing their homes, cars, and even jobs to pay medical bills.

4. THE INSURANCE CRISIS

In the U.S., the healthcare system is dominated by private insurance companies, which decide who lives and who dies based on their financial interests.

- **Expensive Premiums and Limited Coverage:**
    - Even for those who can afford insurance, coverage is limited, leaving many essential treatments out of reach.
    - Additionally, insurance plans often require high copayments and deductibles, which can total thousands of dollars annually before full coverage kicks in.
- **Denials of Payment:**
    - Insurance companies frequently reject coverage requests for costly treatments, citing technical clauses or lack of medical necessity, leaving patients without options.

5. THE REALITY OF THE UNINSURED

For those without insurance, the reality is even more brutal.

- **Declining Public Hospitals:**
    - The few public hospitals in the U.S. are overcrowded and underfunded, often unable to provide adequate care.
    - This forces patients to seek treatment in private hospitals, where they face exorbitant costs or treatment refusals.
- **Free Clinics and Non-Profits:**
    - Some clinics and non-profit organizations try to fill the gaps but their capacity is limited, leaving millions without care.

6. MEDICAL NEGLECT: VICTIMS OF THE SYSTEM

Cases of medical neglect in the U.S. are often tied to financial pressures and cost-cutting measures.

- **Famous Cases:**
    - Patients who waited hours in emergency rooms and died due to delays in treatment.
    - Surgeries performed by unqualified professionals in an attempt to reduce costs.

- **Psychological Impact:**
    - Patients and families affected by neglect often experience profound psychological trauma that lasts far beyond the medical event.

7. FRUSTRATED REFORMS AND THE PATH FORWARD

Although there have been efforts to reform the American healthcare system, political resistance and corporate interests have hindered significant changes.

- **Obamacare:**
    - The Affordable Care Act (ACA), known as Obamacare, was a step in the right direction but still leaves millions without coverage and faces ongoing attacks from opponents.

- **Industry Lobbying:**
    - Pharmaceutical companies, insurance companies, and hospitals spend billions of dollars lobbying to block reforms that could benefit patients.

8. A PROFIT-DRIVEN MACHINE AND INEQUALITY

The U.S. healthcare system is not just a technical failure; it is a reflection of an economic system that prioritizes profit over human life.

- **Profitable Companies:**
    - The largest pharmaceutical and insurance companies report annual profits in the billions, while millions suffer or die due to a lack of medical access.
    - Executives in these companies receive multimillion-dollar bonuses, while patients face debt and despair.

9. CONCLUSION: A SYSTEM THAT CHOOSES WHO LIVES AND WHO DIES

The phrase "pay or die" is not an exaggeration in the context of the U.S. healthcare system; it is a cruel reality. While other developed countries recognize healthcare as a fundamental human right, the U.S. treats it as a consumer good, accessible only to those who can pay.

If the country truly wants to present itself as a global leader in human rights, it must deeply reform its healthcare system, ensuring that no one's life is determined by their ability to pay a hospital bill.

CHAPTER 19: IF YOU FAIL, YOU GO TO JAIL

1. Criminalization of Poverty in the U.S. Bankruptcy System

In the United States, the economic system often punishes those who struggle to navigate its complex financial networks. For the wealthy, bankruptcy can be a strategic tool to protect assets and restart businesses. For the middle and lower classes, however, bankruptcy often leads to financial despair, criminalization, and even imprisonment.

Although bankruptcy is technically a legal measure to alleviate unsustainable debts, its consequences for ordinary people are devastating, transforming a solution into an endless cycle of poverty and punishment.

2. HOW THE SYSTEM WORKS (OR DOESN'T WORK)

- **Differences Between Types of Bankruptcy:**
    - **Chapter 7:** Designed for individuals, it allows the liquidation of assets to pay debts. However, many do not qualify due to strict eligibility requirements.
    - **Chapter 11:** Usually used by large corporations, it allows restructuring of debts while continuing operations. It is largely inaccessible to individuals.
- **Barriers to Access:**
    - Filing for bankruptcy in the U.S. is expensive and bureaucratic, with legal costs that can exceed $2,000 – a sum unattainable for many already in financial trouble.
- **Inexorable Debts:**
    - Certain debts, such as student loans, taxes, and alimony, generally cannot be eliminated in bankruptcy, perpetuating economic suffering.

3. DEBT PRISONS: A RETURN TO THE PAST

Although debt prisons were officially abolished in the 19th century, modern practices have revived this cruel reality.

- **Cases of Debt Imprisonment:**
    - Individuals who fall behind on child support payments can be incarcerated for months.
    - Unpaid fines or court charges often result in arrest warrants.
    - Private companies contracted to collect court debts exploit system flaws to pressure debtors with threats of imprisonment.
- **Judicial Debt Cycles:**
    - In many states, people who cannot pay traffic fines or court fees face imprisonment, creating a cycle where time spent in jail prevents financial earnings to repay debts.

4. REAL CASES: PUNISHING POVERTY

• Clifford's Case: Fines and Imprisonment

Clifford Williams, a low-income worker, accumulated $3,000 in traffic fines and was jailed after failing to pay. His imprisonment led to job loss and worsened his financial situation.

• The Consumer Credit Industry:

Private credit companies often sue debtors and, in some cases, seek arrest warrants for failure to appear in court.

- In 2019, approximately 77 million Americans had collection debt, many of whom faced intimidating lawsuits.

5. RACIAL AND SOCIOECONOMIC DISPARITIES

The bankruptcy and debt system disproportionately affects low-income communities and racial minorities.

- **Alarming Statistics:**
    - African Americans and Latinos are more likely to face creditor lawsuits and have less access to effective legal counsel.
    - In economically depressed areas, predatory loan practices and aggressive collection tactics are more common.
- **Psychological and Social Impact:**
    - Entire families are affected by the stigma, anxiety, and instability caused by judicial debt persecution.

6. Corporate vs. Individual Bankruptcy: A Double Standard

While individuals face harsh consequences, corporations declaring bankruptcy often emerge unscathed or even profitable.

- **Cases of Major Companies:**
    - Companies like Lehman Brothers, during the 2008 financial crisis, declared bankruptcy while protecting executives and shareholders, at the expense of millions of ordinary Americans.
    - Corporate bankruptcy frequently results in massive debt forgiveness and even government subsidies.
- **The Reality for Small Entrepreneurs:**
    - Small businesses face devastating bankruptcies, with owners often losing personal assets and being held

responsible for remaining debts.

7. LONG-TERM IMPACTS ON ORDINARY PEOPLE

For many who go through the bankruptcy system, the consequences extend far beyond the legal process.

- **Post-Bankruptcy Difficulties:**
  - Damaged credit histories limit access to housing, jobs, and future loans.
  - Many spend years trying to rebuild their financial lives, only to be hit again by economic crises or personal emergencies.
- **Health Impact:**
  - Studies show that indebted individuals face high levels of stress, anxiety, and depression, increasing the risk of physical and mental health problems.

8. CONCLUSION: AN UNEQUAL JUSTICE SYSTEM

The U.S. bankruptcy system is more than an economic issue; it is a moral and social failure that criminalizes the poor while protecting the wealthy and powerful.

To change this reality, the country would need to:

- **Reform Bankruptcy Laws:** Make them accessible and fair for everyone.

- **Eliminate Predatory Loan and Collection Practices.**

- **Invest in Financial Support and Education Programs:** Prevent chronic debt issues.

Until these changes occur, millions will remain trapped in a cycle of poverty, demonstrating that, for the less privileged, bankruptcy is not a solution but a social and financial condemnation.

CHAPTER 20: THE TREATMENT OF WOMEN

1. The Barbie Standard: A Cultural Obsession with Beauty and Status

In the United States, the female image is often shaped by an endless pursuit of an ideal of beauty that is frequently unattainable and destructive. This "Barbie Standard," perpetuated by the media, fashion industry, and social networks, prioritizes appearance and popularity above all other qualities.

- **The Unattainable Ideal:**
    - Flawless skin, a slim but curvy figure, perfect hair, and a constant smile.
    - Beauty products, plastic surgeries, and aesthetic treatments promote the idea that perfection is attainable—if you're willing to pay the price.
- **Media Influence:**
    - Hollywood and advertising portray women as objects of desire, reinforcing the notion that their primary role is to please others, especially men.
    - Reality shows and social media foster a culture of constant comparison, intensifying the pressure to meet this standard.

2. Psychological and Social Impact on Young Women

The pressure to achieve this beauty ideal affects women from childhood into adulthood, with severe consequences.

- **Eating Disorders:**
    - Disorders like anorexia and bulimia are

- alarmingly common, particularly among teenagers who internalize the idea that "thinness equals worth."
- Studies reveal that approximately 90% of young women with eating disorders have their body image influenced by the media.

- **Self-Esteem Issues:**
  - Constant comparisons with unrealistic standards lead to feelings of inadequacy and low self-worth.
  - Many women report feeling judged by their appearance before being valued for their skills or personalities.

- **Social Pressures During Adolescence:**
  - The cultural obsession with popularity—being the "prom queen" or the desirable girl—creates a competitive and exclusionary environment.
  - Young women who don't fit this mold often face bullying and social isolation, with long-term consequences.

3. Famous Cases and the Fight Against the Barbie Standard

- **The Body Positive Movement:**
  - Figures like Lizzo and Ashley Graham have challenged conventional ideals, promoting the acceptance of diverse body types.
  - Despite this, criticism and backlash remain frequent, demonstrating slow and resistant progress.

- **Stories of Success and Struggle:**
  - Celebrities like Britney Spears, whose appearance was relentlessly scrutinized by the media, exemplify the emotional damage

caused by public obsession.

- On the other hand, personal acceptance narratives from women like Taylor Swift have inspired many to rethink their relationship with body image.

4. Economic Consequences of Beauty Standards

The imposition of beauty standards is not only a cultural issue but also a billion-dollar industry that profits from women's insecurities.

- **The Beauty Industry:**
  - American women spend an average of $313 per month on beauty products and treatments.
  - Plastic surgeries and aesthetic procedures generate around $20 billion annually in the U.S.

- **Impact on Personal Finances:**
  - Many women go into debt to remain "competitive" in the social and professional markets.
  - This reality perpetuates economic inequality, especially among low-income women.

5. Social Pressures in the Digital Age

With the rise of social media, the "Barbie Standard" has been intensified.

- **Filters and Virtual Surgeries:**
  - Platforms like Instagram and TikTok popularize filters that distort reality, creating a "manufactured perfection" that fuels anxiety and dissatisfaction among young people.
  - Many seek plastic surgery to look like their "edited" social media versions.

- **Influence Culture:**
  - Digital influencers promote a luxurious and flawless lifestyle, often unattainable.
  - This encourages rampant consumerism and reinforces the idea that a woman's value lies in her appearance and social status.

6. Men's Role in Perpetuating the Standard

Although the "Barbie Standard" directly affects women, male validation plays a crucial role in perpetuating this cycle.

- **Unequal Expectations:**
  - Men are not subjected to the same pressures to meet unrealistic beauty standards.
  - Many still evaluate women primarily based on appearance, reinforcing stereotypes and fueling the demand for conformity to the standard.
- **Male Responsibility:**
  - Men who challenge these standards and value women for their authenticity help break the cycle.

7. Paths to Liberation

Overcoming the "Barbie Standard" requires collective effort and profound cultural changes.

- **Education and Awareness:**
  - Promote discussions about body diversity in schools and media.
  - Teach young people to consume media critically, questioning imposed standards.
- **Authentic Representation:**
  - Increase the diversity of body types, ethnicities, and lifestyles represented in media and entertainment.
- **Valuing Real Achievements:**

- ○ Celebrate women for their accomplishments, skills, and contributions to society rather than their appearance.

8. Conclusion

The "Barbie Standard" is more than a beauty ideal; it reflects the social and economic inequalities faced by women. While progress is being made, the path to full acceptance and equality remains long.

As long as culture continues to prioritize appearance over character, society as a whole will suffer—losing not only women's potential but also the opportunity to build a fairer and more inclusive world.

CHAPTER 21: THE NICK FUENTES CASE AND MODERN MISOGYNY

1. **Who is Nick Fuentes?**

   Nick Fuentes is a far-right political commentator and a controversial figure in the United States, known for his incendiary rhetoric, hate speech, and openly misogynistic, racist, and antisemitic views.

   - **Path to Influence:**
     - Emerging as a leader of the "America First" movement, Fuentes uses digital platforms to spread his radical opinions.
     - Despite widespread condemnation, he has gained a loyal following of predominantly young men who share his worldview.

   - **Controversial Statements:**
     - Fuentes has made multiple claims that downplay the importance of women in society, including advocating that they should be subservient to men.
     - He has also suggested that gender equality threatens the natural order, promoting an idealized vision of "traditional roles."

2. **The Reflection of Retrograde Ideas in American Society**

   Fuentes' statements are not isolated incidents but part of a broader current of modern misogyny that has gained traction, especially in online forums and anti-feminist movements.

   - **Internet Hate Culture:**
     - Platforms like Reddit, 4chan, and

> "manosphere" communities amplify misogynistic narratives, fostering hostility toward women.

- Movements such as MGTOW (Men Going Their Own Way) and Incels (involuntary celibates) reflect growing resentment toward female emancipation.

- **Attacks on Female Achievements:**
  - The rise of female representation in politics, the workforce, and education is often criticized by figures like Fuentes as a "threat to traditional society."
  - This creates a climate of resistance to social changes, reinforcing outdated stereotypes.

3. **The Role of Society and Politics**
Fuentes' ideas find fertile ground in a society still grappling with historical gender inequalities.

- **Conservative Rhetoric:**
  - American conservatives often use "protecting traditional family values" as a pretext to attack feminist and LGBTQ+ movements.
  - This reinforces the notion that women should return to subordinate roles, resonating with figures like Fuentes.

- **Misogyny and Political Polarization:**
  - In the polarized U.S. political climate, women's rights are often used as bargaining chips to appease conservative electoral bases.

4. **Consequences of Modern Misogyny**
The perpetuation of these retrograde ideas has profound societal impacts, from mental health issues to real violence against women.

- **Psychological Impacts:**

- The constant devaluation of women in public discourse can lead to diminished self-esteem and a sense of insecurity in social spaces.
- Young men exposed to these narratives develop toxic and hostile attitudes toward women.

- **Increase in Gender-Based Violence:**
  - Modern misogyny is directly linked to rising cases of harassment, psychological abuse, and even femicides.
  - Online anti-feminist movements often glorify violence as a "natural" response to female emancipation.

5. **Notable Statements by Fuentes**

Some of Nick Fuentes' statements highlight his extremist views:

- **On Women in Power:**
  - "If women want equality, maybe they should accept that they're not biologically capable of leading."

- **On Relationships:**
  - "Their role is to serve. It always has been, and it always will be."

  These remarks illustrate a deliberate attempt to delegitimize female achievements and perpetuate structural inequalities.

6. **Society's Reaction and Resistance Movements**

Despite the rise of modern misogyny, there is a growing resistance to these narratives:

- **Female Empowerment:**
  - Movements like #MeToo continue to expose abuses of power and inequalities, creating space for women to share their experiences

and demand change.

- **Countering Hate Speech:**
  - Women's rights advocacy groups are using the same digital platforms to combat hate speech, raising awareness and promoting education.

- **Public Policies:**
  - Some U.S. states are implementing stricter policies to address gender discrimination and domestic violence, though progress remains uneven.

7. **Conclusion**

The case of Nick Fuentes and his inflammatory remarks are symptomatic of a larger issue: the persistence of misogyny in a society still striving for gender equality.

As figures like Fuentes continue to attract attention, it is crucial for society to not normalize their ideas but challenge them with education, empathy, and inclusive policies. The battle against modern misogyny is not just about protecting women—it is about building a fairer and more balanced society for everyone.

CHAPTER 22: FEMINISM AND THE RAPE EPIDEMIC IN THE UNITED STATES

1. The Epidemic of Sexual Violence in the United States

Sexual violence is one of the most urgent and persistent crises in the United States, affecting millions of people every year.

- **Alarming Statistics:**
  - One in six women in the U.S. will be a victim of attempted or completed sexual assault during her lifetime, according to RAINN (Rape, Abuse & Incest National Network).
  - On average, a case of sexual assault is reported every 68 seconds in the country.
  - It is estimated that only 25% of sexual assaults are reported, indicating the issue is even more widespread than statistics show.
- **High-Risk Locations:**
  - American universities are often described as "risk zones," with one in five women reporting sexual assault during their academic years.
  - Additionally, sexual violence is endemic in workplaces, particularly in industries such as entertainment, as revealed by movements like #MeToo.

2. FEMINIST MOVEMENTS: THE FIGHT AGAINST SEXUAL VIOLENCE

Feminist movements have played a crucial role in exposing and combating sexual violence in the U.S., despite facing significant social and cultural resistance over the decades.

- **Key Achievements:**
    - **Violence Against Women Act (VAWA):** Enacted in 1994, this legislation provides legal protection and support for survivors of domestic and sexual violence.
    - **#MeToo Movement:** Initiated by Tarana Burke and popularized by celebrities, this movement exposed the scale of abuse, particularly in Hollywood and politics.
- **Persistent Challenges:**
    - Despite progress, many cases continue to be mishandled by authorities.
    - Gender stereotypes and victim-blaming remain significant barriers to justice.

3. CULTURE OF SILENCE AND IMPUNITY

The sexual violence epidemic is worsened by a culture of silence, shame, and impunity that protects perpetrators and discourages survivors from coming forward.

- **The Judicial System:**
  - Less than 1% of perpetrators are convicted for sexual assault.
  - Many survivors report additional trauma when seeking justice, facing revictimization in court.
- **The Role of Institutions:**
  - Corporations, universities, and even law enforcement agencies have been accused of covering up cases to protect their reputations.
  - A notable example is the scandal involving Larry Nassar, the U.S. Olympic gymnastics team doctor who abused over 150 athletes under the complacent watch of sports authorities.

4. THE IMPACTS OF SEXUAL VIOLENCE

Sexual violence has devastating effects on individuals and communities:

- **For Survivors:**
    - Physical consequences, such as unwanted pregnancies and sexually transmitted diseases.
    - Psychological impacts, including post-traumatic stress disorder (PTSD), anxiety, and depression.
    - Social challenges, such as stigmatization and isolation.
- **For Society:**
    - Sexual violence perpetuates gender inequalities and reinforces oppressive systems.
    - The lack of adequate punishment undermines trust in the justice system.

5. FEMINISM: CHALLENGES AND OPPORTUNITIES

While feminism has achieved significant advancements in the fight against sexual violence, challenges remain.

- **Current Challenges:**
  - **Internal Divisions:** Different strands of feminism do not always agree on the best strategies for addressing issues such as sexual violence and reproductive rights.
  - **Cultural Resistance:** Antifeminist movements, often promoted by figures within the "manosphere," hinder progress.
- **Opportunities for the Future:**
  - **Education:** Implementing comprehensive sexual education programs can help prevent sexual violence from an early age.
  - **Technology:** Digital tools offer new ways for survivors to share their stories and seek support.

6. THE ROLE OF MEN IN COMBATING SEXUAL VIOLENCE

The fight against sexual violence is not solely a women's issue; men have a critical role to play.

- **Education and Awareness:**
    - Men need to be educated about consent, respect, and the impact of their behaviors.
    - Campaigns like "HeForShe" promote the idea that gender equality benefits everyone.
- **Challenging Toxic Norms:**
    - Encouraging men to challenge toxic masculinity norms is essential in preventing sexual violence.

7. CONCLUSION: A SYSTEMIC PROBLEM REQUIRING SYSTEMIC SOLUTIONS

Sexual violence in the United States is not an isolated issue; it reflects systemic inequalities and deeply ingrained cultural values that must be addressed comprehensively.

Feminist movements have been instrumental in shedding light on these issues, but the road to a society free from sexual violence remains long. Through legislative, educational, and cultural changes, the United States can begin to dismantle the rape epidemic and build a fairer future for all.

CHAPTER 23: CRIMES ON AMERICAN HIGHWAYS: THE DANGERS OF THE OPEN ROAD

1. Robberies and Thefts: Vulnerability on the Highways

American highways, often seen as symbols of freedom and mobility, have also become fertile ground for a variety of violent crimes.

- **Abandoned and Stolen Cars:**
  - Drivers experiencing mechanical breakdowns or running out of gas are easy targets. Isolated areas make it difficult to get help quickly, exposing drivers to robberies.
  - Criminals often fake accidents or request assistance to lure victims. Once stopped, drivers are attacked or have their vehicles stolen.
- **Stolen Vehicles and Resale:**
  - Interstate highways facilitate transporting stolen cars to other states, complicating their recovery.
  - In many cases, vehicles are dismantled, with their parts sold on the black market, a crime generating billions annually.

2. Kidnappings and Express Abductions: Terror on the Roads

In addition to thefts, highways have been the setting for even more severe crimes, such as kidnappings and express abductions.

- **Abductions During Long Trips:**
  - Drivers, especially those traveling alone, are frequently approached at gas stations, rest stops, or deserted stretches.
  - Many criminals use weapons to force victims to drive to isolated locations, where they face

physical violence and robbery.

- **Notable Cases:**
    - In 2018, a truck driver was kidnapped by a gang at a rest stop in Nevada. He was held hostage for hours before being rescued.
    - Reports of women being abducted after stopping to help "stranded drivers" are common, often resulting in sexual assault or even murder.

3. The Psychology of Crime on Highways

Highways inherently create an environment conducive to crime:

- **Isolation:** Many stretches are long and deserted, with little to no police surveillance.
- **Crime Mobility:** Criminals can commit offenses in one state and quickly flee to another, hindering police action.
- **Deceptive Appearances:** Criminals often use disguises, such as posing as police officers or stranded motorists, to deceive their victims.

4. Impact on Victims

- **Psychological Consequences:**
    - Survivors of kidnappings or robberies report post-traumatic stress disorder (PTSD), fear of driving, and severe anxiety.
    - For families who lost loved ones to highway crimes, the pain is compounded by uncertainty and the difficulty of obtaining justice.

- **Financial Losses:**
    - Beyond emotional trauma, many victims lose vehicles, belongings, and, in some cases, entire savings during express abductions.

5. The Role of Authorities and Their Failures

Although efforts exist to reduce highway crimes, authorities face significant challenges:

- **Lack of Resources:**
    - Many highway areas lack surveillance cameras or adequate patrols, creating risk zones.

- **Jurisdiction Problems:**
  - Crimes spanning multiple locations create confusion over which police agency should investigate, leading to delays and unresolved cases.

6. Survival Stories

- **Anna's Story:**
  - Anna, a young woman traveling to visit her family in Texas, stopped at night on the shoulder of the road to check a flat tire. She was approached by two men claiming to offer help, but they attempted to rob her. Fortunately, another driver arrived, and the criminals fled.

- **Mark, the Trucker:**
  - Mark was a victim of an express abduction while resting at a stop in Arizona. He managed to escape by hiding his phone and sending a message to the police when left alone in a public restroom.

7. Drug and Weapon Trafficking: Highways as Crime Corridors

Beyond thefts and kidnappings, American highways are extensively used by criminal organizations for drug and weapon transportation. Interstate connectivity facilitates these illicit operations, allowing traffickers to move goods quickly and efficiently.

- **Trafficking Routes: Crime Corridors**
  - **Highways as Primary Channels:**
    - Interstates such as I-95 and I-10 are major routes for drug and weapon transportation.
    - These highways link production areas (like the Mexican border and drug-producing states) to major urban markets in the U.S.
  - **Rural Areas and Isolated Stops:**
    - Rural stretches offer anonymity to traffickers, with less patrolling and

surveillance.

- Remote gas stations and rest areas often serve as meeting points for transferring drugs and weapons.

  - **Notable Cases:**

    - In 2021, a bust on I-40 in New Mexico uncovered over 20 kilograms of heroin hidden in a truck.

    - In Florida, illegal weapons destined for New York's black market were intercepted on I-95, highlighting the scale of criminal activity.

- **How Trafficking Works:**

  - **Drugs:**

    - Narcotics like cocaine, methamphetamines, heroin, and fentanyl are transported in trucks, vans, and even modified passenger cars.

    - Drugs are concealed in secret compartments or mixed with legitimate goods.

  - **Weapons:**

    - Weapon trafficking follows a similar pattern, with arms purchased in states with lenient laws (like Texas and Nevada) transported to stricter states, yielding higher profits.

  - **"Mule" Networks:**

    - Ordinary people, often coerced by debt or threats, are used as "mules" to transport contraband.

8. Police Strategies

Authorities have intensified efforts to curb drug and weapon trafficking on highways but face numerous logistical and legal challenges.

- **Enforcement Methods:**

  - **Highway Patrols:**

- - Officers conduct random stops and inspections in high-risk areas.
    - Drug-sniffing dogs are widely used to detect hidden substances in vehicles.
  - **Checkpoints and Barriers:**
    - Temporary checkpoints are set up on known routes to inspect suspicious vehicles, especially near the Mexican border.
  - **Surveillance Technology:**
    - Cameras and X-ray scanners at toll booths and weigh stations help identify suspicious cargo.
- **Challenges in Combating Trafficking:**
  - **Traffic Volume:**
    - With millions of vehicles on the road daily, it is impossible to inspect all.
    - Traffickers exploit this limitation to operate with impunity.
  - **Sophisticated Tactics:**
    - Use of alternative routes and "invisible" vehicles (trucks with legitimate company plates, for example).
    - Corruption at local levels, where some officials may be bribed to ignore suspicious activities.
  - **Legal Issues:**
    - Many cases are dismissed due to insufficient evidence or procedural errors during seizures.
- **Real Cases and Social Impact:**
  - **Million-Dollar Seizures:**
    - In 2022, a single operation on I-80 in Iowa resulted in the seizure of 50 kilograms of cocaine worth over $5 million.
    - That same year, a convoy on I-20 in Texas was intercepted transporting assault

> rifles to Mexican cartels.
> - **Effects on Communities:**
>   - Trafficking intensifies violence in communities near highways, often serving as distribution hubs.
>   - The ease of transporting weapons also fuels violent crimes in urban and rural areas.

9. Necessary Solutions and Reforms

Despite existing efforts, much remains to be done to combat highway drug and weapon trafficking:

- **Increased Surveillance:**
  - Expand the use of technologies like drones for highway monitoring.
  - Integrate surveillance systems across states to track trafficking patterns.
- **Education and Incentives:**
  - Provide advanced training for highway patrol officers in detection techniques.
  - Offer rewards for reporting suspicious activities on highways.
- **International Cooperation:**
  - Tackling trafficking requires stronger collaboration with countries where drugs and weapons originate or transit, such as Mexico and Colombia.

Serial Killers on Highways: Predators of the Asphalt

American highways are not just routes for transportation but also scenes of brutal crimes committed by some of the most infamous serial killers in history. The anonymity of long, isolated roads provides the perfect environment for predators to exploit the vulnerability of drivers and passengers, turning highways into hunting grounds.

THE CASE OF TED BUNDY: THE MONSTER OF THE ROADS

Ted Bundy, one of the most notorious serial killers in the United States, used highways and secluded areas to lure and abduct his victims. His charm and manipulation skills often helped him gain the trust of young women, frequently pretending to be injured or needing car assistance.

- **Modus Operandi:**
    - Bundy often parked his Volkswagen Beetle in strategic locations like parking lots near highways or park entrances.
    - He would ask young women for help, sometimes pretending to have a cast on his arm or leg.
    - Once the victim trusted him, Bundy would force them into his car, where they were trapped and vulnerable.
- **Highways and Murders:**
    - Many of Bundy's crimes took place near highways, enabling him to escape quickly and leaving authorities with few leads.
    - His murders in states like Utah, Colorado, and Washington demonstrate his strategic use of roads to evade immediate capture.
- **Impact and Lessons:**
    - Bundy showcased how intelligence, charisma, and the tactical use of highways allowed him to commit dozens of murders before being apprehended.
    - His story is a grim reminder of the

vulnerabilities of travelers on isolated roads.

OTHER NOTORIOUS KILLERS: HIGHWAYS AS HUNTING GROUNDS

Bundy wasn't the only one to exploit highways for his crimes. Over the decades, other serial killers have followed similar patterns, taking advantage of the isolation and anonymity of the roads.

- **Samuel Little:**
    - Dubbed the most prolific serial killer in U.S. history, Little confessed to over 90 murders.
    - Many of his victims were vulnerable women, including prostitutes and drug addicts, found near highways.
- **"The I-5 Killer" – Randall Woodfield:**
    - Woodfield terrorized the West Coast during the 1980s, committing a series of rapes and murders along Interstate 5.
    - He used the highway to cover large distances and quickly escape after attacks.
- **"The Highway Killer" – Larry Eyler:**
    - Eyler was convicted for multiple murders of young men and boys during the 1980s.
    - He abducted victims from rest stops and isolated areas along Midwestern interstate highways.

COMMON TRAITS OF HIGHWAY CRIMES

- **Anonymity:**
Highways offer a sense of freedom and anonymity, making it difficult to identify witnesses or apprehend suspects.

- **Lack of Surveillance:**
Many areas near highways, such as rest stops, are poorly lit and rarely patrolled, creating ideal spots for attacks.

- **Vulnerable Victims:**
Serial killers often target individuals traveling alone, with broken-down cars, or in precarious situations like hitchhikers.

- **Mobility:**
Highways allow criminals to travel quickly across state lines, complicating coordination among law enforcement agencies.

THE FIGHT AGAINST HIGHWAY PREDATORS

Authorities have implemented various strategies to tackle the challenge of capturing serial killers operating on highways:

- **Psychological Profiling:**
  Criminal analysts create detailed profiles of suspects based on crime patterns and locations.

- **Tracking Technology:**
  Traffic cameras and toll systems are employed to track suspicious vehicles.

- **Interstate Collaboration:**
  Law enforcement agencies across states work together to share information and track criminals using highways as escape routes.

HUMAN TRAFFICKING

Highways in the U.S. facilitate not only legal transport but also serve as major channels for human trafficking. Often disguised as legitimate transport operations, these crimes exploit the isolation and extensive reach of road networks.

- **Victim Transportation:**
    - Traffickers use regular vehicles like vans, cars, or trucks to blend in with traffic.
    - Victims are often hidden in secret compartments or less visible parts of vehicles.
    - Interstate highways are preferred for their accessibility and ability to cross state lines quickly.
- **Strategic Points:**
    - **Rest Stops:** High-traffic areas with available services help traffickers disguise their activities.
    - **Rural Areas:** The isolation of rural highways reduces the chances of detection.

SOCIAL IMPACT AND RESCUE EFFORTS

Efforts to combat human trafficking include collaboration between government agencies, non-governmental organizations (NGOs), and public awareness campaigns.

- **Government Agencies:**
    - Agencies like the Department of Homeland Security and the FBI work together to investigate and dismantle trafficking networks.
    - State and federal road patrols use surveillance and intelligence systems to monitor suspicious vehicles.
- **NGO Contributions:**
    - Organizations such as the Coalition to Abolish Slavery and Trafficking (CAST) provide legal aid, psychological support, and reintegration services for victims.
- **Public Awareness Campaigns:**
    - Educational efforts teach the public to recognize trafficking signs, such as overcrowded vehicles or suspicious behavior at rest stops.
    - Citizens are encouraged to report anonymously, aiding in the identification of illegal activities along highways.

FATAL ACCIDENTS AND TRAFFIC CRIMES

Highways are also frequent scenes of fatal accidents, some of which conceal deeper criminal activities such as homicide or organized crime.

- **Suspicious Accidents:**
    - Intentional collisions are sometimes used to cover up murders or eliminate rivals.
    - Corporate and political interests may also use highway accidents to silence individuals or divert investigations.
- **Reckless Drivers:**
    - Drunk drivers and fugitives fleeing from law enforcement contribute to the dangers of highways, endangering innocent lives.

CONCLUSION

The dangers of American highways go far beyond traffic accidents. From serial killers to human trafficking and reckless driving, these roads have witnessed countless tragedies. Efforts to mitigate these risks demand increased surveillance, interstate collaboration, and public vigilance to make highways safer for everyone.

CHAPTER 24: HUMAN TRAFFICKING AND ORGAN TRADE

Routes, Trafficking Networks, and the Impact on Victims

Human trafficking and the illegal organ trade remain persistent and alarming problems in the United States. With intricate routes and networks operating both locally and internationally, the country has become a crucial hub for this illicit trade, exploiting social and economic vulnerabilities to profit at the expense of victims.

1. Trafficking Routes and Networks

The United States' strategic location and institutional resources facilitate the operations of human trafficking and organ trade networks. These activities often rely on highways, airports, and international connections to transport victims and illegal goods.

- **Interstate Trafficking Routes:**
  - Human trafficking networks often utilize interstate highways as corridors to move victims.
  - These routes allow traffickers to transport victims across state lines, disguising crimes and evading local authorities.
  - Many victims are lured with promises of work, education, or a better life, only to find themselves trafficked and handed over to criminal networks.

- **International Routes:**
  - The U.S. also serves as an entry and exit point for international human trafficking networks, particularly from Latin America, Europe, and Asia.
  - Airports and ports play a crucial role in clandestine commerce, enabling the transportation of illegal goods and people without

adequate federal and law enforcement oversight.

2. Impact on Victims

The consequences of human trafficking and organ trade are devastating, with victims often facing extreme exploitation, violence, and even death.

- **Sexual Exploitation and Forced Labor:**
  - Women and children are often coerced into the sex industry or forced labor without legal rights or protection.
  - Men are exploited in hazardous and unhealthy labor conditions without compensation or social support.

- **Organ Trade:**
  - Some victims are subjected to illegal medical procedures to extract and sell their organs.
  - These procedures not only pose an immediate threat to victims' lives but often leave them in a state of severe physical and psychological vulnerability.

In some cases, victims are first exploited for labor or sexual purposes and later sold for organ harvesting when they are no longer deemed "useful." This reflects one of the most heinous aspects of capitalism, highlighting why this system can be profoundly harmful to human life.

Scandals Involving Authorities and Corporations

The U.S. has a complicated history of involvement in human trafficking and organ trade, with several cases exposing scandals involving both public authorities and private companies.

1. **Corruption in Government Agencies and Law Enforcement**
   - **Bribes and Collusion:**
     - Law enforcement officers and government officials have been accused of accepting bribes to turn a blind eye to human trafficking.

- Reports suggest that some police officers facilitate the transportation of victims or ignore signs of exploitation in their communities.
  - **Judicial System Failures:**
    - Victims struggle to access legal resources and social support due to the inefficiency and lack of rigor in the judicial system.
    - The legal and penal systems often prioritize economic and political interests over victims' welfare.

2. **Private Companies and Illegal Trade**
   - **Organ Market:**
     - Scandals have implicated medical clinics and laboratories in organ trafficking schemes.
     - Private companies, enticed by high demand and profit potential, have engaged in illegal organ extraction and sales.
   - **Transportation and Logistics Companies:**
     - Transport and logistics companies have been exploited to conceal the clandestine movement of people and illegal goods.
     - Deliveries, stock handling, and daily operations serve as fronts for the covert transportation of victims and illicit products.

Why the U.S. Is a Prime Target for Human Trafficking and Organ Trade

Several social, economic, and institutional factors contribute to the United States' central role in human trafficking and organ trade.

1. **Socioeconomic Vulnerabilities**
   - **Unemployment and Social Inequality:**
     - High unemployment rates and social inequality create opportunities for

> traffickers to recruit victims with promises of employment and financial stability.
>
> - Many individuals from disadvantaged communities fall into these traps, which quickly turn into deadly snares.

- **Minority Vulnerability:**
  - Ethnic and racial minorities, particularly Latin American and African communities, often lack social and governmental support.
  - This makes them easy targets for human trafficking and criminal exploitation.

2. **Strategic Location and Infrastructure**

- **Geographic Proximity and International Access:**
  - The U.S.' proximity to Latin America and access to international markets makes it a central hub for trafficking people and illegal goods.
  - Interstate highways, airports, and ports enable rapid and discreet transportation for these operations.

- **High Internal Demand:**
  - A constant demand for cheap and illegal services perpetuates trafficking in industries such as sex work, forced labor, and organ trade.

Present-Day Trends: Tourist Destinations and Popular Markets

In modern times, human trafficking and illegal organ trade are not confined to rural or isolated areas. They have become increasingly visible in tourist destinations, urban centers, and popular markets, including establishments like Walmart. This reality highlights how deeply human trafficking has infiltrated the social and economic fabric of the United States, creating a disturbing scenario across various aspects of daily life.

1. **Urban Centers and Tourist Locations**
   Traffickers hide their operations in densely populated areas and public venues, taking advantage of constant movement and ineffective oversight.
   - **Tourist Locations:**
     - Hotels, restaurants, and entertainment areas in major cities often serve as fronts for trafficking operations.
     - Victims are recruited from impoverished neighborhoods and transported to these locations for clandestine exploitation.
   - **Shopping Centers and Popular Markets (e.g., Walmart):**
     - Traffickers use large markets as recruitment sites or clandestine meeting points for criminal networks.
     - False job offers lure young people and immigrants into dangerous situations, leading to forced labor or worse.
     - The logistics operations of large retailers are sometimes exploited to disguise illegal transactions.

Conclusion

Human trafficking and illegal organ trade in the United States represent profound and systemic issues that extend beyond clandestine commerce. They involve social, economic, and political challenges, with complicity from public authorities and large corporations perpetuating this brutal reality.

The prevalence of these activities in popular markets, urban centers, and tourist areas exposes the vulnerability of victims and the lack of effective public policies. Addressing this issue requires stronger social control policies, corporate transparency, and significant investment in programs supporting vulnerable communities.

Fighting human trafficking and organ trade is not only a battle against crime but also a commitment to social and moral responsibility. Only through collaboration between the government, civil society, businesses, and communities can victims be protected, and these clandestine operations eradicated, paving the way for a safer and more ethical future for all Americans.

CHAPTER 25: DISAPPEARANCES – A SHOCKING SILENCE
ICONIC CASES AND STARTLING NUMBERS

The disappearance of children and adults in public and tourist areas is a troubling issue in the United States. Among the most impactful cases are Amber Hagerman's abduction, which became a national symbol of child disappearances, and the darker side of seemingly safe and popular locations such as Disney.

1. THE CASE OF AMBER HAGERMAN

Amber Hagerman, a 9-year-old girl, disappeared in 1996 while riding her bicycle in Arlington, Texas. Her body was discovered days later. This tragedy spurred the creation of the AMBER Alert System, aimed at quickly locating missing children.

Social and Familial Impact:

- Amber's case highlighted the shortcomings of social safety nets and law enforcement in protecting children, even in presumed safe environments.
- Many families experience ongoing anguish and frustration due to unanswered questions and insufficient support from authorities when loved ones go missing.

2. DISNEY AND DISAPPEARANCES

Disney, one of the most iconic and frequented tourist destinations globally, has also been linked to disappearances over the years. While its image portrays joy and fun, numerous cases suggest a more sinister reality behind its theme parks.

Disappearances Inside Theme Parks:

- Several families have reported unexplained disappearances within Disney parks. These incidents often occur in high-traffic areas such as Magic Kingdom and Disneyland.
- Evidence frequently points to links with human trafficking networks and child exploitation rings.

3. INDIVIDUALS INVOLVED AND AUTHORITIES' COMPLICITY

Internal Networks and Hidden Facts:

- Investigations have uncovered that some park employees have suspicious connections or criminal histories involving human trafficking and child exploitation.
- These employees, often working with external networks, facilitate clandestine disappearances by targeting vulnerable individuals and concealing their actions from public and official scrutiny.

Systemic Failures of Authorities:

The inefficiency of law enforcement agencies in handling disappearances at prominent tourist locations remains a critical issue. Common problems include:

- **Lack of Thorough Investigation:** High visitor volumes and the complexity of uncovering connections between traffickers and temporary staff often lead to neglected cases.
- **Institutional Protection:** Powerful corporations like Disney wield immense financial and political influence, creating obstacles for police and FBI investigations into potential crimes without clashing with these interests.

Cover-Ups and Complicity:

- Families often face bureaucratic and legal hurdles, with companies failing to provide satisfactory answers about incidents.
- Disney, in particular, has been accused of downplaying incidents and inadequately cooperating with investigations.

4. IMPACT ON SOCIETY

Family Distrust:

Many families have lost faith in places once deemed safe, such as theme parks and popular marketplaces.

Social Pressure and Tourism Decline:

Disappearances negatively affect Disney's image and the broader tourism industry, impacting investments and job creation.

Strengthening of Criminal Networks:

These disappearances fuel underground networks profiting from victim exploitation, playing a significant role in human trafficking and other illegal activities.

CONCLUSION

The disappearance of people in the United States, particularly in seemingly secure and popular locations like tourist attractions and urban markets, exposes the intricate and severe nature of this social and criminal issue. Iconic cases, such as Amber Hagerman's tragedy and the unsettling reports from Disney parks, underline how clandestine networks and institutional corruption enable human trafficking and the systematic vanishing of victims.

A genuine, transparent effort involving families, the government, society, and major corporations is imperative to combat these criminal operations. Investments in preventative measures, corporate accountability, and greater transparency from authorities could help address these challenges and protect countless Americans and international visitors. The safety of children and families must not be compromised for corporate interests or financial gain—it is a fundamental ethical and social obligation that American society must confront without delay.

CHAPTER 26: CRIMES ON HALLOWEEN – THE REAL-LIFE TERROR

Introduction

Halloween, originally a pagan holiday celebrated to ward off evil spirits, has become a cultural symbol in the United States—a day of costumes, parties, candy, and fun. However, behind the festive facade lies a dark reality: real crimes and chilling incidents. Despite the colorful costumes and decorations, Halloween exposes societal vulnerabilities and institutional failures. This chapter delves into famous historical cases and modern crimes, revealing how this date reflects cultural and institutional fragilities in the U.S.

Famous Cases

1. **Ronald Clark O'Bryan – The "Candy Man"**

   One of Halloween's most infamous cases is that of Ronald Clark O'Bryan, known as the "Candy Man."

   - **The Case:**

     In 1974, O'Bryan poisoned Halloween candy in his Texas community. He laced chocolates with cyanide and handed them out, intending to collect life insurance money.

   - **Outcome:**

     He tragically killed his own son, Timothy O'Bryan, in this calculated and heartless act.

   - **Impact:**

     This case raised concerns about the safety of Halloween treats and prompted communities to adopt measures like inspecting candies before allowing children to consume them.

2. **Masked Murders and Crowds**
The anonymity provided by costumes during Halloween often facilitates heinous crimes. Masked perpetrators blend into crowds, making it easier to commit murders and evade capture.

- **Notable Cases:**
Criminals have frequently used masks and costumes to attack unsuspecting victims. Crowded urban celebrations, such as street parades, exacerbate the chaos, complicating law enforcement efforts.

3. **Disappearances and Abductions on Halloween**
The festive atmosphere of Halloween often serves as a backdrop for mysterious disappearances, particularly involving children and teenagers.

- **Party and Street Risks:**
Abductions often occur during parties or on busy streets where children are vulnerable.

- **Challenges for Authorities:**
The difficulty in identifying suspects and the inefficiencies in investigations often leave these cases unresolved, causing ongoing anguish for families.

Modern Crimes

1. **Rise in Crime and Vandalism**
Contemporary Halloween celebrations are often marred by acts of vandalism, physical assaults, and hate crimes.

- **Public Destruction:**
Groups frequently engage in destructive behaviors, such as breaking windows, vandalizing walls, and damaging property.

- **Conflicts and Assaults:**
Clashes among groups in urban and suburban areas have become common, particularly during large-scale parties.

2. **Child Exploitation and Abuse**
   Concerns about child abuse and exploitation during Halloween festivities have grown in recent years.

   - **Informal Events and Groups:**
     Children are often coerced into selling candy, performing in unsafe environments, or becoming vulnerable to human trafficking.

   - **Community Safety Risks:**
     Lack of adequate protective measures in community events leaves young people exposed to potential harm, especially in major urban centers.

Conclusion

While Halloween is meant to be a day of celebration and fun, it also exposes profound societal and institutional vulnerabilities in the United States. The combination of costumes, crowd culture, and the anonymity of masks makes Halloween particularly dangerous, testing the effectiveness of preventive measures and public safety agencies.

A robust and collaborative approach involving civil society, governments, and communities is essential to implement efficient surveillance, community inspections, and alert systems. Investments in preventive policing and the strengthening of community networks are crucial to protect both children and adults, preventing Halloween from becoming a day of tragedy and loss.

The challenge lies in balancing cultural celebration with respect for personal safety, ensuring that Halloween remains a unifying day of joy and not one of fear and despair. Only through rigorous preventive measures and societal commitment can the U.S. restore Halloween's spirit as a day of community celebration rather than a harbinger of real-life terror.

CHAPTER 27: THE MARKETING OF THE AMERICAN DREAM

Introduction

The American Dream is a concept so deeply ingrained in the culture of the United States that it has become almost a national mantra. It promises success, freedom, and prosperity through hard work and personal initiative. Hollywood plays a crucial role in perpetuating this myth, using films and series to craft an idealized image of life in America. The message is clear: in the United States, anyone can achieve success regardless of social background, race, or financial condition. However, what the media and propaganda conceal is the harsh reality of a socioeconomic system that benefits only the wealthiest and most powerful, while the majority struggle to survive. This chapter examines how Hollywood and the media contribute to constructing this myth and how, in practice, the system perpetuates inequality and exclusion.

1. Hollywood as a Propaganda Tool

The Image of Instant Success

Hollywood films and series often depict characters who achieve success and wealth quickly and effortlessly. These portrayals of the American Dream frequently feature stories of individuals rising from obscurity to become millionaires or gaining instant fame through talent or luck.

- **Examples of Impact:**
  - *Cinema and Music Icons:*
    Many believe that being discovered by an agent or appearing on a reality show is the gateway to financial success and fame. The underlying message is clear: anyone can succeed if they believe in themselves and put

in the necessary effort.

- ○ *Entrepreneurship and Business:*
  Films like *The Pursuit of Happyness* epitomize the idea that hard work leads to success, while conveniently ignoring the roles of social connections, initial investments, and financial resources—privileges accessible only to a select few.

The Power of Social Media and Influencers

With the advent of social media, Hollywood is no longer the sole purveyor of this propaganda. Public figures and influencers now reinforce the idea of the American Dream through curated lifestyles.

- **Influencers and Promises:**
  Everyday individuals share stories of instant success, luxurious trips, and quick earnings, overlooking the systemic financial challenges faced by those without similar resources.

- **The Overemphasis on Appearances:**
  Success is often linked to appearance and excessive consumption. Social pressure to own the right car, wear designer clothes, and live in lavish homes pushes people toward materialism rather than personal development or financial stability.

2. Constructing a Myth

The Reality of Socioeconomic Inequality

The American Dream promises social mobility through hard work, but the reality is starkly different. The economic system in the United States is riddled with inequalities.

- **Winners Take All:**
  Billionaires and large corporations control the bulk of the nation's wealth. Access to investments, education, and social networks is concentrated among the financially and socially privileged.

- **Barriers to Success:**
  For most, achieving the American Dream requires initial capital, social connections, educational resources, and financial stability—elements typically reserved for the privileged few.

The Manipulation of Social and Political Narratives

While promoting individual success, Hollywood simultaneously upholds a political and social system that benefits the elite.

- **Corporate and Political Partnerships:**
  Major studios and celebrities often maintain ties with politicians and corporations, influencing decisions that favor capital and big businesses at the expense of workers and underserved communities.

- **Erasure of Social Issues:**
  Critical issues such as unemployment, racism, poverty, and violence are either downplayed or addressed superficially, distorting the real American experience.

Conclusion

Through its stories and imagery, Hollywood serves as a primary tool for constructing the American Dream—a dazzling and enticing, yet often deceptive, illusion. The portrayal of easy and universal success obscures the reality of a system that privileges only those with financial and social power.

The true American Dream should be built on a system where equal opportunities are not just theoretical but tangible for all. Achieving this requires effective public policies, investments in education and social infrastructure, and dismantling barriers that perpetuate the dominance of corporations and the wealthy at the expense of the rest of society.

Instead of being a myth that excludes and marginalizes, the American Dream must become a collective commitment to providing real access to progress, success, and dignity for everyone, regardless of social background, race, or initial circumstances. Hollywood must evolve from being merely a propaganda machine to becoming a platform for authentic stories that challenge inequalities and inspire genuine social and economic progress accessible to all.

CHAPTER 28: THE HARSH REALITY BEHIND THE MASK

1. Social Inequality

The Gap Between the Rich and the Poor

In the United States, the image of prosperity and progress often portrayed by the media and Hollywood is just the tip of the iceberg. The social reality is marked by deep and persistent inequality, with an ever-widening gap between those with wealth and those without.

• Disproportionate Wealth Distribution:

According to economic studies, a small fraction of the American population controls the majority of the country's wealth. Approximately 1% of the population holds around 40% of the nation's wealth, while the poorest 50% own just 2% of the assets. This means most resources and opportunities are concentrated in the hands of a few, while the majority struggles to meet basic needs.

• Lack of Social Mobility:

Although the myth of the American Dream suggests that anyone can achieve success through hard work, the reality shows that social mobility is limited. Factors such as family background, education, and connections significantly influence a person's future. Many remain trapped in a cycle of poverty that seems impossible to break.

The Role of Corporations and Public Policies

• Corporate Lobbying and Inequality:

Large companies and corporations wield significant control over political and economic decisions in the U.S. Through powerful lobbying, they secure tax benefits, incentives, and policies that favor investors at the expense of workers and communities.

• Flawed Public Policies:

Government social programs and initiatives often fall short of ensuring a dignified life for the poor. Limited social assistance and insufficient investment in educational and community programs create a scenario where the poorest are consistently marginalized.

2. LACK OF PSYCHOLOGICAL AND PHYSICAL WELL-BEING

The U.S. healthcare system is largely privatized and based on direct payments or health insurance, making healthcare a luxury that is often out of reach for those without sufficient financial resources.

• Expensive Health Insurance:

Most Americans rely on private health insurance, which can consume a significant portion of their income. Workers with low-paying jobs or without benefits struggle to access adequate medical care.

• Medical Neglect and Lack of Access to Treatment:

Hospitals and clinics often prioritize profitability over patient welfare, leading to superficial treatments and medical neglect. Millions face financial hardships just to access essential care, such as medical consultations, surgeries, and treatments for chronic illnesses.

Mental Health Issues Exacerbated by Consumerism

The lifestyle associated with excessive consumption and materialism in the U.S. significantly impacts the mental health of its citizens.

• Social Pressure and Depression:

The relentless pursuit of success and material possessions creates constant social pressure. Many are led to believe their happiness depends on social status and possessions, resulting in anxiety, depression, and feelings of failure.

• Isolation and Loneliness:

Extreme individualism in American culture devalues community support and interpersonal relationships. Many live in isolation, lacking social or emotional support, further exacerbating mental health issues and making it harder to seek help.

3. THE CLASS SYSTEM

A Society Structured by Wealth

In the U.S., the idea that only those with financial power deserve a dignified life lies at the heart of its social and economic system. Society is structured to generate wealth only for those at the top, while the poorest are often left with no real prospects for advancement.

• Barriers to Entry:

Access to quality education, decent housing, and stable career opportunities requires considerable financial resources. Without these, the path to progress is limited, and dreams of success often remain illusions.

• Culture of Merit and Exclusivity:

The myth of the American Dream promotes the idea that success and merit are achieved solely through individual talent and effort. However, this concept ignores the reality that access to the best schools, professional networks, and opportunities is often restricted to those who already possess wealth and power.

The Exclusion of Marginalized Communities

• Systemic Discrimination:

African American, Latino, and Indigenous communities face additional barriers due to systemic discrimination and structural racism. This is evident in challenges accessing jobs, education, and adequate healthcare.

• Lack of Public Investment:

Many of these communities live in neglected neighborhoods without proper infrastructure, quality schools, or access to essential resources. This perpetuates a cycle of poverty and social exclusion that is difficult to break.

CONCLUSION

The mask of American society, promoted by the media and consumer culture, hides the profound social and economic inequality that affects millions daily. Hollywood and the media may present the American Dream as a path to progress and success, but the reality is a system that benefits only the economic elite and marginalizes those without resources or connections.

True social and economic progress in the U.S. requires profound structural changes, investments in public education, robust social assistance, and policies that ensure real opportunities for all. This means addressing class disparities, fixing the broken healthcare system, and combating systemic racism that has long affected historically marginalized communities.

As long as the country continues to pursue profit and extreme individualism, the promise of the American Dream will remain an empty myth—a compelling tale that excludes, divides, and destroys those who, despite their best efforts, never had a real chance at success and dignity.

CHAPTER 29: IMMIGRANTS – THE OTHER SIDE OF THE "DREAM"

1. Inhumane Treatment of Immigrants

Detention Centers and Dehumanizing Conditions

Immigrant detention centers in the United States are often described as true *"fields of suffering and abandonment"*, where human rights are violated, and people's dignity is ignored.

- **Overcrowding and Lack of Resources:**
  Many centers are overcrowded, with insufficient space for detainees. This creates a chaotic and dangerous environment where hygiene and public health are compromised. Prisoners face a lack of proper food, medical care, and basic sanitation.

- **Forced Labor:**
  In many cases, immigrants awaiting deportation are subjected to forced labor, receiving extremely low wages or no pay at all. They are often placed in dangerous and exhausting activities, disregarding basic worker rights.

- **Human Rights Violations:**
  Human rights organizations have reported cases of physical and psychological abuse, medical neglect, and restrictions on personal communication for immigrants. The absence of translators makes communication difficult, and many detainees do not have access to adequate legal assistance.

Deportation and Social Hostility

The deportation policy implemented in the U.S. has been severe and often brutal, especially in recent years.

- **Aggressive Deportation:**

Immigrants, regardless of how long they have lived in the U.S. or their contributions to society, can be deported at any time, sometimes without prior notice. Many deportations separate families, leaving children and parents in a state of despair.

- **Hostility and Structural Racism:**
American society presents a scenario of social and institutional hostility and prejudice against immigrants. Often seen as competitors in the labor market, responsible for wage decreases and increased unemployment rates, immigrants face a racist and xenophobic narrative promoted by politicians and media that devalues immigrants and sees them as *"intruders."*

2. THE MESSAGE OF EXCLUSION

The "American Dream" as an Exclusive Privilege

The American Dream, often depicted as a promise of success and prosperity through hard work, does not include all immigrants. The exclusivity of this dream is a reflection of social and economic policies that prioritize only those who already have access to the system's resources and privileges.

- **The "System of the Privileged":**
  The reality is that only those with documentation, financial connections, or social privileges have access to quality educational opportunities, stable jobs, and healthcare. This creates a system where economic success is tied to existing financial and social conditions rather than true merit and universal opportunity.

- **Legal and Administrative Barriers:**
  Immigrants face a bureaucratic maze where documentation required to access services and jobs is complex and often unattainable. This keeps them in temporary and poorly paid jobs without guarantees of basic rights or future stability.

Social Exclusion and Stigma

In the U.S., immigrants are often targets of social stigmas and stereotypes, which create an additional barrier between them and acceptance in American society.

- **Xenophobic Narratives in Media:**
  Many media outlets perpetuate negative stereotypes about immigrants, associating them with crime, drugs, and social problems. This creates a distorted and negative public perception that distances the population from immigrants and weakens

community ties.

- **Social Exclusion and Racism:**
Immigrant communities often live in poor urban or suburban areas where access to employment and education is limited. This prevents young people from these communities from having real opportunities for social and economic progress, creating cycles of poverty and violence that are difficult to break.

3. THE EXCLUSIVITY OF ACCESS TO PROGRESS

Social Structure and Economic Disparity

In the United States, the social structure is designed to favor the wealthy, leaving immigrants and low-income workers at a constant disadvantage.

- **Systemic Economic Inequality:**
  Investments and economic policies often benefit large investors and corporations, while social programs intended for workers and immigrants are either cut or inadequately maintained. This means that economic progress is exclusive to those who already possess capital and connections.

- **Limited Social Mobility:**
  Despite promises of equal opportunities, social mobility is limited for those without the necessary financial support. Access to higher education, good jobs, and investments is often a luxury reserved only for those at the top of this social structure.

Exclusion in the "Dream"

- **Citizenship and Limited Rights:**
  For many immigrants, citizenship means an unstable future and limited access to social and economic system benefits. They do not have the right to compete on equal terms in the labor market and face additional obstacles in legal and economic systems.

- **Need for Structural Reforms:**
  The solution to this social and economic exclusion requires comprehensive reforms, such as fair immigration policies, investments in public education and robust social programs, along with ethical

corporate practices that include immigrants as part of the workforce under fair and equitable conditions.

CONCLUSION

The American Dream, often presented as an ideal accessible to anyone willing to work hard, has proven to be a myth for many immigrants in the U.S. The reality for them includes dehumanizing detention centers, complex bureaucratic barriers, harsh deportation policies, and a society that marginalizes them both socially and economically.

While media and Hollywood perpetuate an image of boundless progress, the exclusion of immigrants highlights the urgent need for inclusive structural changes. This means breaking institutional barriers, reforming the healthcare and social assistance system, combating systemic racism, and ensuring truly equal opportunities.

Only through these changes can the American Dream become a real and accessible concept for everyone, without excluding those who, despite adversity, seek only a dignified life and the chance to contribute to American society.

CHAPTER 30: FREEDOM OF EXPRESSION OR HATE SPEECH?

1. The Fallacy of Freedom of Expression

The New Excuse for Extremism: The Nick Fuentes Case

In the United States, freedom of expression is one of the foundational pillars of the Constitution, but paradoxically, it has often been used as a shield by those who promote extremist and prejudiced rhetoric. Nick Fuentes, a far-right influencer and commentator, is an emblematic example of this reality. He represents the dilemma between protecting freedom of expression and the hate speech that seeks to create social divisions and intolerance.

- **Using the Constitution as a Shield:**
  Fuentes and other extremists frequently claim that their opinions are protected by freedom of expression and, therefore, cannot be questioned or suppressed. He promotes racist, misogynistic, and xenophobic ideas, claiming that he is simply exercising his constitutional right to speak freely.

- **Social Media and Radicalization:**
  Social media platforms play a crucial role in this scenario. Platforms like Twitter and YouTube, while defending freedom of expression, also enable extremist content to gain traction and followers. This creates a space where prejudiced speech and extremist ideas circulate freely, making it difficult to combat such content.

GROUPS OF EXTREMISTS AND THE LEGAL SHIELD

Besides figures like Nick Fuentes, several extremist groups in the U.S. use freedom of expression as a legal justification for their activities and rhetoric.

- **Extremist Organizations:**
  Supremacist groups, neo-Nazis, and far-right organizations use freedom of expression to organize protests and events, often in public spaces and with the protection of laws that guarantee their constitutional rights.

- **Legal Protection:**
  American courts, based on their commitment to individual rights, struggle to restrict these speeches. Freedom of expression is a fundamental and sacred right, but the limit only arises when speech incites violence or poses real threats to society.

2. The Hypocrisy Behind "Freedom"

The Exclusivity of True Freedom of Expression

Although the Constitution protects freedom of expression, in practice, it is often restricted when speech targets vulnerable groups, such as women, ethnic minorities, and LGBTQ+ individuals.

- **Inciting Prejudice and Discrimination:**
  Often, rhetoric promoting misogyny, racism, and homophobia not only offends but also creates systemic environments of discrimination and physical violence, particularly among young people and marginalized communities.

- **Social and Psychological Impact:**

Hate culture and verbal attacks against social minorities have profound effects on self-esteem and psychological well-being. This strengthens social exclusion and creates a cycle of discrimination and resentment among different groups in American society.

3. THE CHALLENGE OF REFORMS AND THE SEARCH FOR BALANCE

Regulating Social Media

The debate about regulating social media is ongoing in the United States, but the challenges are significant.

- **The Platform Dilemma:**
  Companies like Facebook, Twitter, and YouTube uphold individual freedom but, at the same time, become spaces where hate and intolerance thrive. Algorithms that prioritize content with higher engagement end up promoting extremist ideas and polarizing audiences.

- **Attempts at Control and Legislation:**
  Various bills have been proposed to restrict speech that incites violence and hate, but there is resistance, both from extremist groups and technology companies themselves. Balancing freedom and social responsibility remains an ongoing and critical challenge in this debate.

EDUCATION AND SOCIAL CULTURE

To combat the spread of hate speech, a commitment to education and cultural development is essential, promoting values of inclusion and respect from an early age.

- **Inclusive Educational Programs:**
  Educational initiatives can help combat prejudice by teaching children the importance of diversity and respect for differences from an early age.

- **Influence of Celebrities and Cinema:**
  Hollywood and pop culture also play a crucial role in shaping social opinions. Celebrities and influencers can use their influence to challenge extremist narratives and promote representation and inclusion, helping to shape more respectful and diverse social values.

CONCLUSION

Freedom of expression in the United States, although a sacred constitutional right, exists in an unstable balance between protection and social responsibility. This balance has been exploited by extremist figures like Nick Fuentes, who hide behind legal shields to propagate hate speech. However, true freedom of expression should not be a space where prejudice, misogyny, and xenophobia can thrive.

A social and political commitment to structural reforms, greater accountability from social media platforms, and inclusive educational initiatives is essential. Only through these changes can the United States genuinely uphold fundamental rights, ensuring an environment where individual freedom coexists respectfully and equally, making the American Dream a real and accessible promise for all, without space for exclusion or intolerance.

CHAPTER 31: HOLLYWOOD UNMASKED

1. Scandals Involving Directors and Actors

Abuse and Manipulation: The Dark Side of the Backstage

Hollywood, known for its glamorous image and high-impact entertainment, hides many dark secrets. Behind the cameras and red carpets, the American film industry has been marked by cases of abuse of power, sexual harassment, and manipulation, involving both renowned directors and acclaimed actors.

- **Harvey Weinstein: The Symbol of Power and Abuse**
  The case of Harvey Weinstein represents one of Hollywood's largest scandals. The influential former producer, known for producing iconic films like *Pulp Fiction* and *Shakespeare in Love*, was accused of multiple cases of sexual harassment and assault, involving various famous actresses over the decades. The #MeToo movement, which gained momentum in 2017, brought to light many victims who exposed Weinstein and other powerful names in the industry.

- **The Role of Major Studios:**
  Hollywood studios, in many cases, turned a blind eye to abusive behaviors, protecting directors and actors in the name of financial success and the industry's prestige. This mindset allowed abuse to continue for years without significant consequences.

- **Legal Challenges:**
  Judicial efforts to hold perpetrators accountable are complicated. Many cases involve confidential financial settlements, where victims accept large sums of money in exchange for silence—a scenario that perpetuates abuse without adequately punishing the

responsible parties.

2. CHILD ABUSE AND CONTROVERSIAL CASES: NICKELODEON AND P. DIDDY

Nickelodeon and the Case of Children

Nickelodeon, one of the leading television networks for children and teens, also faced significant controversies regarding child abuse. Various cases emerged over the years, involving children and teens who worked in the entertainment industry and claimed they were exploited and abused behind the scenes.

- **Testimonies and Allegations:**
  Many former child actors and technicians, after leaving the entertainment scene, revealed toxic environments and excessive exploitation by directors and producers, where financial interests took precedence over the emotional and physical well-being of children.

- **Pressure and Excessive Exposure:**
  Children were often subjected to long recording schedules and, in many cases, faced psychological and emotional pressure to meet high performance and professionalism expectations. This led to deep physical and psychological traumas, affecting these children both personally and professionally.

Sean Combs (P. Diddy) and Music Scandals

Sean Combs, also known as P. Diddy, is a well-respected name in American music and entertainment. However, he is also associated with scandals involving children and teens, particularly in the rap and hip-hop scene, where fame and success come with a high price.

- **Exploitation and Discrimination:**

Accusations about the excessive use of child talent and the pursuit of financial profit at the expense of young artists frequently emerge in P. Diddy's and others' entertainment circles.

- **Abusive Contracts:**
Many early artists speak about contracts that kept them tied to abusive agreements, receiving only a small fraction of the profits while industry giants accumulated substantial wealth.

3. WHY DOES HOLLYWOOD EMBRACE THIS DARKNESS?

Culture of Success and Waste

Hollywood prioritizes financial success and fame above everything else. The pursuit of popularity and quick profits often results in neglecting ethics and respect for human rights.

- **Careers at Risk:**
  Many actors, technicians, and young talents who entered the industry with dreams of success end up being exploited and discarded without support or protection from studios and companies.

- **Influence of Sponsors:**
  Investors and sponsors also play a crucial role in maintaining this scenario, as they are more focused on short-term financial returns than on long-term reputational impacts.

Internal Networks and Hidden Power

In Hollywood, the influence of contracts, personal relationships, and confidential agreements creates an internal power system that is difficult to penetrate.

- **Silencing Mechanisms:**
  The use of private financial agreements, exclusive contracts, and relationships between studios and agents creates an environment where public denunciations are easily suppressed.

- **Lack of Oversight Mechanisms:**
  Regulatory agencies often have limited power to intervene and hold those managing the backstage affairs of this industry accountable, which allows Hollywood to remain a space where exploitation and excessive power coexist.

CONCLUSION

Hollywood, despite its global cultural influence and glittering image, is a microcosm of the ethical flaws and social disparities present in American society. Abuses involving powerful directors, child exploitation, and complicated relationships between contracts and financial interests reveal structural problems within the entertainment industry.

These scandals demonstrate how the pursuit of fame and financial success often overrides respect for dignity, ethics, and human rights. The industry requires profound structural reforms, both in institutional policies and interpersonal relationships, ensuring that financial success is built on ethical values and respect for human talent and professionalism, rather than on exploitation and sacrifice.

CHAPTER 32: WILD CAPITALISM AND INEQUALITY

1. CAPITALISM AS A TOOL FOR CONCENTRATING WEALTH

The Rise and Domination of the Capitalist System in the USA

Capitalism in the United States began shaping the American economy from the early days of colonization and industrialization. However, over the years, this system has evolved into a wild capitalism, where accumulating wealth is no longer just a goal but a means of maintaining social and economic structures in favor of the powerful and large corporations.

- **Power of Corporations:**
  In the American landscape, large corporations such as Amazon, Google, Apple, and Microsoft dominate the economy and concentrate a significant portion of national wealth. Only the executives and shareholders of these companies amass fortunes that surpass the budgets of many countries.

- **Disregard for Workers:**
  Wild capitalism largely operates on low wages, mass layoffs, and temporary contracts, focusing solely on profit. This means many American workers struggle to secure housing, healthcare, and a decent quality of life.

- **Gig Economy and Precarious Jobs:**
  Technology and transportation companies, like Uber and Airbnb, have created the concept of temporary and flexible employment. However, these jobs come with financial insecurity and a lack of social benefits, making economic stability nearly impossible for many.

EXPORTING THE CAPITALIST MODEL

The United States has not only implemented this system internally but has also exported it globally.

- **Influence of Foreign Policies:**
  With the help of global financial institutions like the IMF and the World Bank, the USA has imposed neoliberal policies in various countries, encouraging privatization and market liberalization. The goal was to ensure American corporations' control over global resources and markets.

- **Unequal Trade Agreements:**
  Trade agreements like NAFTA ensured that American products dominated the markets of neighboring countries, especially Mexico, while simultaneously destroying jobs and local industries. This strengthened these countries' dependence on American capitalism and guaranteed wealth flow to the USA, while most people in other countries faced unemployment and poverty.

2. THE IMPACT ON POOR AMERICANS' LIVES

Internal Economic Inequality

In the USA, wild capitalism has resulted in extreme social and economic inequality, where the poor are often ignored by the system, and resources are concentrated in the hands of a few.

- **Employment Issues and Poverty:**
  Over 12% of Americans live below the poverty line, and many workers, even with stable jobs, struggle to pay rent, purchase medications, or secure basic food supplies.

- **Debt and the American Dream:**
  The American dream, which promises social ascent through individual effort, has become an illusion for many. University students, burdened with educational loans, face years or even decades to pay off their debt, limiting their economic and social opportunities.

- **Lack of Access to Healthcare:**
  The private healthcare system in the USA exacerbates the situation for the less privileged. Many people lack access to necessary medical care, and treatments depend on health insurance, which not everyone can afford. Capitalism imposes a cruel choice: pay for medical services, or die.

THE DEVALUATION OF MANUAL AND TECHNICAL WORK

Wild capitalism in the USA values intellectual and technological work but often devalues manual and technical work, such as construction, transportation, and maintenance.

- **Unequal Wages:**
  Professionals in these fields, essential to the basic functioning of society, like drivers and technicians, receive modest salaries and do not have the same rights and benefits as workers in specialized or corporate sectors.

- **Social Stigma:**
  American society holds a stigma against manual work, associating it with a lower social status. This creates a cultural barrier that discourages many young people from considering careers that are crucial to the country's infrastructure and economic functioning.

3. THE GLOBAL IMPACT OF WILD CAPITALISM

Inequality Between Countries

The impact of American capitalist policies is not limited to the domestic landscape; it extends globally.

- **Underdeveloped Countries and Exploitation:**
  Countries in Latin America, Africa, and parts of Asia face significant challenges due to the capitalism exported by the USA. Often, these countries are exploited as sources of raw materials and resources but do not receive substantial investments in infrastructure or social development.

- **Human Trafficking and Slave Labor:**
  The relentless pursuit of cheap production in the USA has led to the growth of human trafficking and inhumane working conditions, especially in factories located in countries with weak labor regulations. This creates a cycle where capitalism fuels exploitation and poverty both in American and international territories.

EXORBITANT DEBT AND EXTERNAL DEPENDENCE

Many countries that followed the path of neoliberal policies imposed by the USA have accumulated significant external debt, becoming dependent on American financial decisions.

- **Global Financial Institutions:**
  The IMF and the World Bank, often influenced by American interests, end up being used as tools of economic control, ensuring the submission of developing countries to the power of American corporations and their investors.

- **Imbalanced Development:**
  The result is a world where wealth is concentrated in a few places, while many countries and people face a lack of basic resources, poverty, and social instability.

CONCLUSION

Wild capitalism, a system initially designed to create opportunities and prosperity, has become a system that relentlessly concentrates wealth, disregarding fundamental values of equality and social justice. In the United States, this system creates a landscape where only those with resources and power thrive, while workers and the less privileged are often left marginalized.

Globally, the capitalism exported by the USA has created a network of dependency, exploitation, and inequality, where entire countries are subjugated to the interests of American corporations and international financial institutions.

Significant changes are urgently needed, both in the United States and globally, with economic policies that promote fair resource distribution, equal opportunities, and real investments in healthcare, education, and social welfare. The true promise of the American dream—success and progress accessible to all—will only be fulfilled when capitalism ceases to be a system that serves only the powerful and instead becomes a system that respects and values the effort and talent of everyone, ensuring a sustainable and equal future for all society.

CHAPTER 33: THE PRICE OF POWER

1. Global Domination and the Cost of American Decisions

Over the decades, the United States not only built its image as a global superpower but also shaped the world stage through political, military, and economic decisions. However, these decisions came at an exorbitant cost — both for Americans and the rest of the world. The power and influence that the U.S. exercises over other countries were often achieved through war, economic exploitation, and political manipulation, leaving a trail of destruction and suffering.

• Wars and Military Intervention:

American history is marked by military interventions that not only changed the course of other nations but also destabilized entire regions. From the Vietnam War to Iraq, and the prolonged presence in Afghanistan, the costs of these operations go far beyond the battles themselves. Thousands of civilians and soldiers lost their lives, cities were devastated, and psychic trauma persists for generations.

• International Economic Exploitation:

Through international agreements and multinational corporations, the U.S. exploited the natural and human resources of less developed countries. American companies dominate markets, impose unfavorable working conditions, and secure colossal profits, while host countries face poverty and underdevelopment.

2. POLITICAL MANIPULATION AND INFLUENCE ON GLOBAL DECISIONS

The U.S. also shaped the world by manipulating global political and economic structures, often using international institutions and agreements as instruments of control.

• Influence in International Organizations:

Organizations like the United Nations, IMF, and World Bank are often used as vehicles for American influence. While they claim support for development and aid, in practice, their decisions frequently reflect the interests of American elites at the expense of the needs of developing countries' populations.

• Manipulative Foreign Policy:

From the CIA to secret political deals, the U.S. leveraged intelligence and economic power to overthrow leaders in foreign countries and establish governments that served only corporate and economic interests. Examples include supporting the military regime in Chile during the 1970s and influencing Middle Eastern countries, where strategic interests and oil dominated political and military decisions.

3. EXPLOITATION OF THE MASSES AND THE SOCIAL COST

Internal Social Inequality and Domestic Conflicts

American power and influence came with significant costs for the American population as well. The relentless pursuit of political and economic control generated an internal landscape of social inequality and fragmentation.

• **The Lives of the Poor and the Absence of Social Safety Networks:**

Many American families live in poverty without adequate access to healthcare, education, or stable employment opportunities. This occurs because the system is designed to favor investors and corporations, leaving less privileged communities at the mercy of economic hardships.

• **Psychological and Social Issues:**

Individual success and the competitiveness exacerbated by capitalism resulted in a society with high levels of stress, anxiety, and depression. The pressure to always stay ahead, the fear of job loss, and constant comparisons of material possessions contribute to the deterioration of social relationships and mental health.

• **Culture and Distorted Values:**

Promotion of Materialism and Superficiality:

American culture, largely propagated by Hollywood and advertising, promotes extreme consumer values and materialism. This creates the false idea that success is equated with wealth and social status. Such a view distorts personal objectives and fosters superficial and self-interested relationships.

Lack of Purpose and Depersonalization:

Many people live in pursuit of purely material success without a real purpose or meaningful contribution to society. This leads to emotional emptiness and the breakdown of human connections, which are the foundation of any truly prosperous society.

4. THE PATH TO REFLECTION AND GLOBAL JUSTICE

Global Responsibility:

The consequences of American power and influence cannot be ignored. Now is the time to look at the past and analyze history, learning from mistakes and the outcomes of decisions made in the pursuit of economic and political power.

• Global Accountability:

As one of the most influential nations on the planet, the U.S. must take responsibility for repairing the damages caused worldwide. This means respecting human rights, strengthening international aid policies, and investing in developing countries to ensure that resources and opportunities are distributed fairly and equitably.

• Reevaluation of Social and Economic Values:

Internally, it is necessary to reform capitalism, transforming it into a system that prioritizes people's well-being over absolute profit, ensuring universal access to education, healthcare, and stable employment.

CONCLUSION

The power of the United States is both a symbol of influence and control and a warning of the consequences of capitalism and excessive power. This power was built at the cost of people's lives — both Americans and others who suffered under American decisions on the global stage.

The true strength of a nation lies not only in its ability to dominate markets and armies but in its capacity to create equitable, just, and collaborative societies, both domestically and internationally. The next chapter, *"The Price of Power,"* will delve deeper into how the United States can and should work to repair these damages, with a genuine commitment to global justice and respect for human rights — a necessary reflection to finally establish a system where power brings real and lasting progress, not just for the few, but for everyone.

CHAPTER 34: THE ILLUSION OF THE AMERICAN DREAM – THE FINAL MESSAGE

A Promise That Never Materializes

Throughout this book, we have analyzed the dark and hidden elements behind the myth of the "American Dream." Sold to the world as a symbol of freedom, success, and opportunity, this dream conceals a system that benefits only the powerful, while the majority is left behind. The truth is that, in the United States, the promised dream is often just a mirage — a carefully constructed illusion designed to sustain a system that perpetuates inequality, exploitation, and manipulation.

The U.S. has sold itself to the world as the place where anyone, regardless of origin or social condition, can achieve fame and fortune solely through hard work. However, the reality for millions is quite different:

- **Persistent Poverty and Growing Inequality:**
  While billionaires accumulate astronomical wealth, millions of Americans live in precarious conditions, without access to proper housing, healthcare, or education. Access to a promising future is not guaranteed but rather a privilege reserved for the few.

- **Media Manipulation and Propaganda:**
  Hollywood, advertising, and American media are used as propaganda tools, creating false images and unrealistic standards that pressure people into pursuing success based on materialism and superficiality. This often results in loneliness, anxiety, and emotional emptiness.

- **Violence and Social Instability:**

Human trafficking, highway crimes, international economic exploitation, and the inhumane treatment of immigrants are just some of the issues that illustrate how the American system is built to serve the interests of the elite, at the expense of workers, minorities, and less privileged communities.

The Real Cost of Freedom and Success

True success and freedom should be based on values of equality, respect, and real opportunities for everyone, but the American system fails to deliver this. Instead, we see:

- A distorted freedom of speech, where hate speech is disguised as individual rights.
- A private healthcare system that excludes many but only enriches those who control it.
- Companies that exploit resources and people in the name of profit, disregarding community well-being and the environment.

This is the reality that the U.S. sells as the "American Dream" — a scenario of glory, opportunities, and progress that, in practice, becomes a nightmare for those without the same resources and privileges.

The Need for Reflection and Transformation

It is time to question the narrative sold by American media and propaganda. We must look at the facts, understand history, and take action. We should strive for a future where:

- Success is not a privilege reserved for a few, but a basic right for everyone.
- Opportunities are accessible regardless of social origin, race, or gender.
- True power is used to promote social justice, respect for human rights, and sustainability.

Each of us, no matter where we are, has the power to question, resist, and demand change. A commitment to justice, ethics, and human dignity should be pursued, not just by those in power, but by society as a whole.

FAREWELL TO READERS

We have reached the end of this journey — but reflection and learning should not stop here. This book is just an invitation for you to question, analyze, and seek answers about the society we live in and the system we are part of.

May you, the reader, continue to question what is shown, investigate the truth behind the images sold by media, and fight for a more equal and just world. Let us all work together to transform what is called the "American Dream" into a real commitment to social progress, mutual respect, and the well-being of everyone, not just a privileged few.

Thank you for accompanying this journey. May your reflections and actions contribute to a future where power brings real and lasting progress, where success is a right, and where freedom truly belongs to all, free of illusions and masks.

Until we can create a system that reflects our real values — solidarity, justice, and progress — may our eyes and hearts remain open to the truth.